THE
QUICK
& EASY
COOKBOOK

VENTURA BOOKS
New York City

Printed in the United States
All Rights Reserved

INTRODUCTION

"Brother, can you spare a dime..."

Anyone who has gone shopping recently knows that old song, "Brother, can you spare a dime..." is grossly out of date. In these times of soaring inflation, a dime, in some cities, will still get you a phone call cross-town, but that's about all. At this point, the old Depression classic might better be updated, "Brother, can you spare a dollar..." In fact, since the time when that song was written, food prices have actually shot up more than 700%!

It's no longer just "the poor" who have trouble putting a good, hot, nutritious meal on the table every night...it's a problem for everyone now. And there seems to be no end in sight to the jolting prices that are being slapped onto almost every kind of edible in existence.

In spite of the big bite that inflation takes out of every dollar you earn, there is a solution. And that's exactly what this book is all about.

There are many paths you can take toward fighting inflation...coping with rising food prices...and feeding your family. As a matter of fact, you can probably eat as well as you used to, and spend less to do it, too!

INTRODUCTION TO SHOPPER'S TIPS

You could be a great homemaker, and still not know some of the simplest ways to cut down on your shopping, cooking, and serving expenses. Though common sense and imagination play a big part in creative economizing on family meals, you also need to know the tricks of the trade. These are the inflation fighting methods that have developed over the years, with the help of smart housewives and professional economists, as a way of stretching your food budget. This section, Shopper's Tips, goes beyond helping you make ends meet. It not only gives you an entire system of money-saving plans and ideas, it also gives you additional tips which will further lower your food budget and cooking expenses. In fact, you may find that after following the guidelines set up in this section, you'll be eating better than ever before, while actually spending less money on your grocery bills.

Shopper's Tips starts by saving you money even before you get to the market! In this section you'll learn how to plan your meals around both your family's needs and the advertised specials, you'll learn about comparison shopping and which stores are best for what products. You'll also learn about list-making, impulse buying, the do's and don't's of coupon clipping, and much more.

This section equips you for the deluge of products and prices that you'll find in just about any market, and helps you weed out the good deals from the bad. You'll learn how to use unit pricing, rainchecks, bulk-buying, store brands, and even the generic brands being offered in many stores at substantical savings.

Packaging is the foe of any home budgeter, and you should know how to bypass it...in the produce aisle, at the canned vegetable shelf, in the frozen foods freezers, etc. Shopper's Tips tells you exactly what will give you less while costing you more...and how to avoid all of it.

Developing ingenuity and imagination is an essential for anyone trying to cut food and cooking costs, and that includes knowing where the leftovers from this meal are going to fit into your next meal. Should you serve them as is, or combine them for a totally different effect? That's something for you and your family to consider in planning a meal.

Shopper's Tips also helps you to build an awareness of your own food consumption style. Does your family eat too much? Are they overstuffed and undernourished? Did you know that Americans, as a people, are more overweight than ever before? These are the many areas that Shopper's Tips covers, to help you save money while shopping, and to help you enjoy meals more with every penny you save!

READ THE SPECIALS IN THE PAPER

You can begin saving money before you even begin to shop. How? Read the specials in the papers which contain the Food Section for the grocery stores and supermarkets in your area. In this section you will see full-page ads on what's on sale at various stores that week. You'll also find money-saving coupons for the week, like a gallon of milk for $1.19 with a $10 purchase and the clipped coupon from the paper. Other items are listed so you can compare store prices. By reading the specials in the paper every week you can save quite a bit of money. You'll also become much more familiar with prices—and learn how to know a good deal when you see one.

PLAN YOUR MEALS AHEAD OF TIME

The next thing you do, after reading the paper, is plan your meals around the week's specials. If hamburger or chuck steak is on sale, you can create meals around those items by fixing meat loaf or pot roast that week. By planning a little beforehand, you can save yourself time and money. And it is worth the few minutes of effort if you are on a budget or have a family to feed.

MAKE A LIST

Along with planning your meals based on the week's specials, it is always a good idea to make and take a grocery list with you to the store. Before you make your list, check your cupboards, refrigerator, and freezer, and see what you have and what you need. With the list in hand, you'll know the necessary items you should buy. You can, of course, be flexible and buy other items besides what's on your list, but making a list gives you a solid foundation or plan to work with when you are confronted by aisles and aisles of items. It also helps to limit impulse purchases.

ONCE IS OFTEN ENOUGH

It's a good idea to try shopping for everything once a week. Besides, who wants to spend every day in the grocery store picking up something for dinner? After you have checked the papers that week, noted the specials, planned your menus, and made a list, go to the store on Wednesday or Thursday and stock up. Friday nights after work are the worst at the supermarkets. The lines are long and the baskets are piled high. This can turn shopping into a real chore. Unless you enjoy crowds it's always best to shop at a less crowded time. By shopping for all your big purchases once a week, you save time and energy. And most important of all, each time you enter the store, you are likely to purchase items on impulse which drives up your bills. And that brings us to another point.

DON'T IMPULSE BUY

This can kill your budget. Taking a list decreases this possibility, but it is something you will have to guard against. Buying on impulse can give you an odd assortment of expensive items you cannot use or coordinate in your menu planning for the week. Each time you pick up an item that is not on your list, stop and ask yourself: "Do I really need this?" It's a good way to get you to put some of that merchandise back on the shelves.

DON'T GO TO THE STORE HUNGRY

Always eat before you shop. Going to the store on an empty stomach is a mistake. Research shows that people spend less on their grocery bill if they shop on a full stomach. It seems that not so many of those foods look quite so tempting and it cuts down on impulse buys. Try going to the store after you've eaten, you'll see you're not so apt to buy one of everything you want to taste at the moment!

LEAVE THE KIDS AT HOME

Many items are packages especially to attract the attention of children. There can be nothing harder on your budget than members of your family begging for expensive extras not on the list. They especially love the cookie section and the cereal aisle. When something strikes their eye, they want it. And that can lead to a stand off. What's likely to happen? You'll make the purchase just to please them.

CLIPPING COUPONS

A housewife from New Jersey, now nationally known as the "Coupon Lady" says she saves $2,500.00 a year on food by simply using coupons, manufacturer's refund offers and smart shopping techniques. $2,500.00 a year in after-tax dollars—that's a lot. Those coupons you may have been ignoring are worth quite a bit of money.

Therefore, it's a good idea to start using them. You can find coupons in the mail, in magazines and in the newspaper. Clip and save them for the items you use. $2,500.00 a year is a nice bonus.

COMPARE PRICES— EVEN WITH COUPONS

Refund offers are a type of reimbursement for buying certain products. The manufacturer pays you for buying his product by refunding the purchase price (or sending you $1.00 or a gift in return for sending him so many boxtops, labels, weight circles or wrappers) after you've used it. If you're using these products, it will only cost you a stamp to send for the refund. All you have to do is save the proof of purchase and write away for your refund. These refund offers are written on the packages themselves, or advertised in magazines and newspapers. Be sure to look for them.

BE A COMPARISON SHOPPER

Shop the various stores in your neighborhood to see which ones have the better bargains on what products. Don't develop a loyalty to one store just because it's convenient. Experiment. You may be surprised at how prices vary in the same location. One store may have better prices on dairy products, one on meats, and another on canned goods. It is good to know and remember to buy those items where the prices are better.

If a certain store has better prices and it is only a few blocks further, it is worth your effort to investigate and shop there. Of course, if the store is ten miles away, then you must consider the cost of getting there, plus your extra time.

KNOW WHERE TO SHOP FOR WHAT

Supermarkets

Supermarkets usually deal in such large volume that they can afford to sell products cheaper than the local neighborhood grocery store that has limited stock and fewer customers. You pay for that convenience as they are still open when everyone else is closed. Shop there only when you must and purchase *only* those items that are a real necessity. Don't buy on impulse at a convenience store!

Ethnic Neighborhoods

Depending on where you live, there are other options available for shopping. If you live in a metropolitan area, try the ethnic neighborhoods for fresh vegetables, spices, breads, fish and certain meats. Italian and Chinese neighborhoods sometimes have very low prices on those items that are used in their traditional cuisine. These places are often fun to browse through as they are full of variety and color and you may be surprised to learn that some of the products are quite a bit lower in price than at the supermarket.

Farmer's Markets

Farmer's markets are also fun to visit. The prices are generally lower too. Here you'll find fresh vegetables, fruits and other wares in open-air stands where you can pick and choose what you want.

Roadside Stands

If you live in the country or are driving that way, stop and check out the roadside stands along the highway. Here you will find a variety of fruits and vegetables much cheaper than in the city grocery stores.

A note of warning: If you do make roadside purchases, make sure you bring along a food storage chest for any perishables. Country fresh eggs aren't much good if they've spoiled from the heat on the ride home.

There are also places where farmers will let you pick your own. These are occasionally advertised in the local paper. But most are advertised by word of mouth or signs along the roadway. In these orchards and gardens you can take your family and baskets and pick all you want of tomatoes, strawberries, apples, blackberries or whatever. These are fun and you are charged by the basket, bushel or peck. And the prices are very kind on your pocketbook.

Food Cooperatives

Another place where prices are lower are food cooperatives. Here you must join and become a member for a low fee or in exchange for some volunteer help at the co-op. Prices here are wholesale. There are neighborhood co-ops, women's co-ops, university co-ops, vegetarian co-ops, farmers' co-ops, and many others. See if there is one in your area. Some of these are advertised on local bulletin boards or in local papers for new members.

MISCELLANEOUS SPOTS

Other places to shop are thrift shops, warehouses and factory outlets. Here products are drastically reduced. At thrift shops the products may be a day old, but the prices are slashed from 50% to 75%. Warehouses have dry goods in bulk at substantial savings. Factory outlets sell certain products—baked goods, linens, shoes, clothing. You can see if any of these are in your area and then determine the quality of the products and compare the prices.

BUY BY THE UNIT

Utilize unit pricing to your advantage. Unit pricing is required by law in some states. Most of the larger stores have the signs below the product which state exactly how much you are paying per ounce or per pound for that particular item. You may notice that one item which appears to be priced lower than another is actually costing more per ounce than another brand.

CHECK OUT "HOUSE BRANDS"

Most major stores or grocery chains have their own "house brands" which are much lower priced than nationally advertised brands. Read the ingredients and compare the prices. They are usually similar in quality and taste to the national competition.

LOOK FOR THE "WHITE LABEL"

These are generic foods and they are now available in most stores. These are in the line of canned goods like vegetables and jams and jellies. The difference is that the items used are of "standard" quality rather than "choice" quality. Some of the vegetables may be of different sizes and have a few stems or uneven cuts mixed together. But they are satisfactory and would be excellent choices for soups and stews or casserole dishes. Best of all—they are generally priced up to 40% below many other brands.

THINK BIG

When you do your weekly shopping, try to buy the items that you use frequently in bulk or larger quantities. The savings are generally considerable as the larger sizes are priced lower than the smaller packages, because you are paying as much for the packaging and handling costs. Staples like flour, rice, sugar, coffee, tea, soap, detergent, and paper products are cheaper in the large quantities and you don't have to worry about spoilage. It works the same for pet food. If you own a dog or cat, and buy a certain brand of pet food, it is better to buy the 20 or 50 pound size than to buy the small 5 pound bag every few days.

DON'T BUY NON-FOOD ITEMS
IN THE GROCERY STORE

It is usually better economy to look for non-food products in discount or drug stores rather than grocery stores. The prices are more likely to be discounted because it's their specialty. The grocery store handles these items more often as luxury items.

When you go to the drug store ask for generic brands on drugs and prescriptions if available. These are of identical quality but do not have a familiar brand name. You pay extra for knowing the name. Be sure to ask your doctor, when he writes the prescription, if you can buy the generic drug. And, if it's non-prescription, be sure to ask your pharmacist for the generic brand.

YOU BE THE BUTCHER

Meats, which use most of your budget dollars, are high enough, but their costs can be shaved considerably if you buy meats whole and cut them up yourself. Whole chicken is cheaper than cup up fryers, for instance. You pay the butcher's time and service. Buy whole and do your own work. Hamburger is better priced in quantities over 5 pounds, so take it home and divide it yourself into various portions for meatloaf, individual patties or one pound servings. If you need pork chops, buy the loin roast section and cut individual chops.

If you have a freezer, buy meat in bulk from a butcher, or buy it from a meat packing house, if there is one close by. If you buy your meats from the same butcher (after you compared quality and prices) he will usually tip you on what is a good price buy or what is especially nice that week.

FOOD FOR ALL SEASONS

By nature, vegetables and fruits are usually lowest in price in the summer months. During the winter you pay a lot more for the transportation costs that truck fruits and vegetables to cold areas of the United States. So, in the summer, take advantage of the abundance by eating lots of green leafy salads and having fresh fruit for dessert. Also, you might want to consider canning and freezing some of those glorious fresh fruits and vegetables for use in colder months.

FRESH IS CHEAPER THAN
FROZEN OR PACKAGED

Fresh fruits and vegetables are generally cheaper than those canned and frozen. Again, you are paying for the labor charges. Check the prices and compare. Packaged fresh and dried or canned items are higher priced and generally not as tasty as the fresh variety. Try to keep it simple. Remember, the less packaging...the less labor costs...the less middlemen...the better price at the checkout line.

AVOID DIETETIC FOODS

There is a high premium on any kind of "special" food. You're paying for someone not to add sugar or salt or some other ingredient. So, you are paying more money for less goods. If you want dietetic foods, try to make them yourself.

STAY AWAY FROM SOFT DRINKS

Colas are high priced mixtures of water, sugar, food coloring, carbonation and caffeine. They are not that good for you, your teeth, or your food bill. Try to stay away from them. Learn to drink natural fruit juices, seltzer water...or best, plain water.

DON'T LET SNACKS EAT YOUR BUDGET

Be on guard when you go through the aisles of snack foods. They are tempting, but expensive—and fattening. Keep them out of the house. If you must, buy popping corn and make it at home. (And it's kinder to the waistline, too). It is a good source of fiber and relatively low in calories if you do not add salt or go heavy on the butter.

BEWARE OF CONVENIENCE FOODS

A lot of foods are ready made now. All you need to do is add water, or an egg and pop them in the oven. They are popular because they are easy and quick, and look homemade. But read the prices and ingredients. You are paying a lot for extra convenience, not to mention the chemicals and preservatives. Some things are tastier and healthier made from scratch.

READ THE DATES ON PERISHABLES

Dairy products, especially, have a time limit in which they must be sold and used. These are often on the container, either on the top or on the side. Look for these when you buy them. Buy only enough so that you can use them before their expiration period. Food that rots or spoils in your refrigerator is wasted money.

CHECK OUT MERCHANDISE WHICH IS MARKED DOWN

Often stores will have a shopping cart full of items marked down. These often are cans which are slightly bent or the labels are partially removed. Look for these in the store and see if you need any of these items. (However, never buy or use a can that's swollen.)

ASK FOR RAINCHECKS

Special items often sell out quickly. Ask the manager if there are any left. If not, ask for a "Raincheck." The manager will write a "Raincheck" for that item, at the special price, to be used the next time you shop at the store. Don't be embarrassed to ask. If they advertise the item for a special price, it's your right to get it, even if they sell out.

RETURN BAD MERCHANDISE

Sometimes you will buy merchandise that is not acceptable. (The milk may have turned or the bread gone stale.) Don't just throw them away disgusted. Take them back to the store with your receipt and ask for a refund.

They will write a purchase exchange or give you your money back.

DON'T BE SHORTCHANGED
AT THE CHECKOUT LINE

After all this saving with coupons and specials, keep a close watch on the cash register. Sometimes cashiers don't know about special prices on particular items and will charge you the full price. Watch the register and keep your receipt tape. Cashiers make mistakes too. Count your change. It has been known to happen that you are given the wrong change or charged too much.

IMAGINATION STRETCHES
YOUR BUDGET

A restricted budget doesn't mean you need to eat poorly. A little imagination can be a great way to create interesting and appealing low-budget menus. Presentation is important. The nicer something looks, generally, the better it will taste. Food should appeal to your senses—smell, sight and taste. Experiment with herbs and spices, they are a wonderful way to perk up the flavor. Paprika adds color and zest to fish and chicken and egg dishes. Garlic and oregano make Italian dishes smell even more wonderful and awaken your tastebuds.

Also, try ethnic dishes for variety. Often, they are relatively inexpensive to fix because they use less meat, or less expensive cuts. You can go Chinese one night and have Chicken with Vegetables. You can go Italian and have spaghetti, with sausage and garlic bread.

When you do experiment, try to stick to recipes you know your family will like. Avoid the purchase of a lot of strange ingredients you will only use once.

LEARN, MAKE AND DO

One way to combat inflation is to learn to do things yourself. That might mean deboning your own chicken, stuffing your own pork chops, making your own apple sauce, gravies, whipped cream and french fries. There are a lot of items you can make at home that are cheaper than the ready made store bought kind, and taste a lot better, too.

THE ART OF SUBSTITUTION

You can substitute certain products for others and be amazed how good they are. For example, substitute non-fat dry milk in recipes, or mix it with whole milk. It's not only very good, and economical, but it's also lower in cholesterol. Use plain yogurt in place of sour cream for dips and on potatoes. Make your own yogurt very inexpensively using non-fat dry milk, regular milk and yogurt culture. Use less expensive proteins for large quantity meals like chicken or tuna, cheese or eggs, to replace more expensive proteins like beef or lobster.

RECYCLE YOUR LEFTOVERS

Stretch out your meals and your food budget by learning to make good use of leftovers. Remaining vegetables from a meal can be used for soups and stews. If not used right away, they can be frozen. Even the water from cooking or blending vegetables (which contains most of the vitamins), can be used as a marvelous soup stock. Or, feed it to your plants, they thrive on it. Combine leftover meat and vegetables in a new way for casseroles or pot pies.

Use the "whole food". Stems of broccoli, leaves of celery are very good in soups. Sweetened syrups from canned fruits can be saved and used. Make desserts, puddings—even boil it down to make pancake syrup!

The tail end of cereals, pretzels, potato chips and bread crumbs can be salvaged for stuffing, toppings for casseroles, and added to meatloaves and meat balls.

Leftover turkey, beef, or chicken can be creamed over toast, cut into strips over salads, put into soup or stock, mixed with gravy for hot sandwiches, mixed with sauce over noodles, or diced into its own salad.

Leftover pancake batter can be mixed with meat or vegetables and deep fried for fritters.

The lonely heels of bread can be used for stuffing or for bread pudding.

Coffee grinds can be recycled too. Dry them out. Then put them in the oven for a few minutes. They are ready to use again and still have that fresh roast taste.

The peelings of oranges and lemons are very useful and shouldn't be thrown in the garbage. Grate the lemons and oranges and store in a jar. These will keep indefinitely and can be used as flavoring in baking or as toppings.

Leftover orange juice from the breakfast table can be put in ice cube trays and frozen for use as popsicles for the children.

Leftover potato salad can be fried in a skillet and converted into hash browns for breakfast.

Leftover hot dog buns can be cut into strips, sprinkled with spices, and heated in the oven to be changed into breadsticks.

Stale bread can be changed back to fresh soft bread by sprinkling it with water, wrapping it in foil, and placing it in the oven for a short time.

DON'T COOK FOR AN ARMY

If you are cooking for two, don't buy and prepare enough for eight, unless you plan to use all those leftovers. Too often, people make the mistake of over-estimating the amount of food needed and cook too much. They often don't make use of the leftovers, pushing them further back into the refrigerator until they find the leftovers sprouting a life of their own, and then have to throw them out. Try to buy only what you think you'll use.

MAKING YOUR OWN DESSERTS

You can save money by making desserts and snacks at home. For instance, make your own popcorn for watching TV or going to the drive-in movies. Make lemonade or iced tea instead of buying sodas at the store. Use crushed ice from your refrigerator and pour fruit juice over it for snow cones for the kids.

Caramel or candied apples, perfect snacks in the fall, can be made just as easily at home. Popcorn balls are easy and inexpensive to make, too. You can also make your own cakes and cookies instead of buying them at the bakery. Leftover icing can be placed between shortbread or biscuits to make sandwich cookies.

STORING AND KEEPING FOOD

It is important not to waste food. Learn to store food properly. When you place items in the freezer, put the expiration date on the package so you know how old it is. Some items have a tendency to get lost in the freezer and then are tasteless or have freezer burn. Meats can be frozen for up to six months before the taste and quality goes bad.

Items such as lettuce or apples go bad quickly if they have any brown spots appearing on them. Remove these before you store them. The rest will keep much longer.

BAG IT

You can also save by using what's in your refrigerator and brown bagging your lunch to work or school. It is much cheaper than eating in a restaurant where prices can range from $1.00 to $5.00 just for a sandwich.

Besides lunch, you can take meals and snacks from home for drives, picnics and the beach.

Inviting friends over for pot luck suppers is both fun and an inexpensive way to get together. Everyone brings a different dish and you enjoy a buffet of wonderful specialties at very little cost.

GROWING YOUR OWN

Another way to beat the high cost of living is to grow it yourself. If you have a yard, then you can have a garden for the price of a few seeds and some good exercise tilling the soil. You can grow your own vegetables and herbs for delicious summer meals.

If you do not have access to any land, you can still have a window garden where you can plant in pots a few tomatoes or peppers or herbs. Dill, sage, parsley, rosemary and thyme are easy to grow on your kitchen window sill. When you need fresh herbs, just snip a few sprigs.

BRING HOME THE BACON

If you or your spouse is so inclined, you can "catch" the main course. If you like to fish, nothing is better than fresh out of the water. If there's more than you can eat, freeze it.

If you are a hunter too, the menu can be even more varied. In season, rabbit, squirrel and grouse are very tasty if prepared properly. If you enjoy hunting, it is one sure way to save on food bills.

APPETIZERS

PATE

2 lbs. calves' liver
1/2 lb. chicken livers
2 eggs, beaten
1/2 C heavy cream
2 T lemon juice
1 tsp garlic salt
4 T brandy
4 slices bacon, cooked and crumbled

Put livers through finest blade of food grinder. Add all other ingredients except brandy and bacon. Mix well. Warm the brandy in a small saucepan. Ignite and pour over liver mixture when flames subside. Pack liver into a well greased loaf pan. Cover pan tightly with aluminum foil. Place loaf pan in large shallow pan containing 1-1/2 inches of water. Bake in a 325°F. oven for two hours. Remove from oven and remove foil. Weight the pâté with a heavy object that will cover loaf. Chill overnight. Unmold on bed of greens and top with crumbled bacon.

Serves 10 to 12.

ANTIPASTO ROLLS

1 can (8 oz) pitted black olives
1 jar (4 oz) Italian roasted red peppers
1/4 lb. thin sliced Prosciutto

Drain olives and peppers. Cut peppers into 1-inch strips. Lay slice of Prosciutto flat. Center a strip of pepper on each slice of meat. Put olive at one end of meat slice and roll jelly-roll fashion. Fasten with toothpicks.

Makes about 15 rolls.

COCKTAIL MEATBALLS

1 lb. lean ground beef
2 T onion, minced
1 C fine cornflake crumbs
1 tsp cornstarch
1/2 tsp salt
1/4 tsp pepper
1/8 tsp allspice
1 C milk
Oil for deep frying

Mix all ingredients except oil thoroughly. Form into small balls about 3/4 of an inch in diameter. Let stand for 15 minutes. Heat oil in frying pan to 375° F. Deep fry meatballs for 1-1/2 to 2 minutes. Drain on absorbent paper. Serve hot with toothpicks.

Makes approximately 60 meatballs.

HAM AND CHEESE AMERICANA

1/2 C dairy sour cream
1/2 C mayonnaise
1/4 tsp dry mustard
24 slices cold boiled ham
6 slices American cheese, each cut into 4 lengthwise strips
24 stuffed olives

Combine dairy sour cream, mayonnaise and mustard. Lay ham slice flat. Spread with some of the sour cream mixture. Lay strip of American cheese on one end of ham slice. Roll jelly-roll fashion. Fasten with toothpick topped with olive.

Makes 24 rolls.

TANGY HAM ROLLUPS

1-1/2 C flour
1-1/2 tsp baking powder
1/2 tsp salt
1 C Cheddar cheese, shredded
1/2 C butter
1/4 C cold water
8 thin slices boiled ham
Mustard

Sift the flour, baking powder and salt into a mixing bowl.
Combine with cheese and butter. Gradually add water, stirring
with a fork, until dough sticks together. Knead on floured
surface 10 times. Divide dough in half and roll out each half on
floured surface to a 10 x 14-inch rectangle. Cut each rectangle
into four 5 x 7-inch pieces. Place a slice of boiled ham on each
piece of dough. Spread lightly with mustard. Roll jelly-roll
fashion, starting at the narrow end. Seal edge. Place seam-side
down on a greased cookie sheet. Bake in 450° F. oven for 10 to 12
minutes, until golden brown. Remove from oven, cut each roll
into 5 or 6 slices and serve while hot.

Serves 8 to 10.

CHICKEN PINEAPPLE SPREAD

1/4 C crushed pineapple
1/2 C chicken, cooked and minced
3 T mayonnaise

Drain pineapple and reserve liquid. Combine all ingredients
and mix well. Thin mixture to desired consistency with
pineapple juice. Spread on crackers or toast squares.

Makes approximately 1 cup.

PERSIAN CANAPES

4 T mayonnaise
16 2-inch rounds of white bread
32 small or medium-sized shrimp, cooked and shelled
1 2-oz. jar black caviar
1 hard cooked egg yolk, sieved

Spread mayonnaise lightly on bread rounds. Place 2 shrimp in center of each. Surround with border of caviar and dust lightly with egg yolk. Cover with plastic wrap and refrigerate until ready to serve.

Makes 16 canapes.

WAFFLES A LA RUSSE

1 recipe waffle mix
1/2 C sour cream
1 4-oz. jar caviar

Prepare waffle mix as directed on package. Drop batter from a tablespoon on to a greased, heated, waffle iron for small round waffles. Be careful not to let waffles touch. When done, put aside. Just before serving reheat in 350°F. oven for 5 minutes. Top each with sour cream and caviar.

Makes about 25 small waffles.

MUSHROOM PUFFS

1 can (4-1/2 oz) deviled ham
24 assorted crackers
1-1/2 C Cheddar cheese, grated
3/4 C mayonnaise
1 can (4 oz) button mushrooms, drained

Spread ham on crackers and place in broiler pan. In a small mixing bowl combine the cheese and mayonnaise. Spread on top of deviled ham. Top with button mushrooms. Place under broiler for about 1 minute, or until the cheese mixture bubbles and becomes slightly brown.

Makes 24 puffs.

BUBBLY CHEESE AND BACON

1/2 lb bacon, cooked
3/4 C American cheese, shredded
1/4 C butter, softened
Toast rounds

Crumble cooked bacon and mix together with cheese and butter. Spread on toast rounds. Line cookie sheet with aluminum foil. Place rounds on cookie sheet and broil about 4 inches from heat until cheese melts and bubbles. Remove from broiler and serve while still hot.

Makes about 50 pieces.

AVOCADO SPREAD

2 ripe avocados
3 T lemon juice
1/4 tsp salt
1/4 tsp seasoned pepper
2 strips bacon, cooked and crumbled

Peel avocados and mash with lemon juice. Add salt, seasoned pepper and crumbled bacon. Mix well. Use as spread on crackers or rye rounds. May also be used as a dip with chips, pretzels, or fresh carrot sticks or celery.

SESAME PINWHEELS

1 C flour
1-1/2 tsp baking powder
1/2 tsp salt
1/4 C shortening
1/3 C milk
1/4 C green onions, finely chopped
2 T sesame seeds

Sift the flour, baking powder and salt into a large mixing bowl. Cut in shortening until particles are the consistency of cornmeal. Add milk and stir just until thoroughly moistened. Roll out dough on floured surface into a 20 x 12-inch rectangle. Sprinkle with green onion and sesame seeds. Roll up, starting with the long edge. Seal edge well. Cut into 1/2-inch slices and place flat on greased cookie sheet. Bake at 450°F. oven for 10 to 12 minutes, or until golden. Serve warm.

Serves 6 to 8

LITTLE KOREAN OMELETS

1/4 pound very lean, double ground round steak
1 green onion, finely chopped; use a little of the green
1 clove garlic, finely chopped
2 tablespoons white sesame seed (available in most spice sections)
1/4 teaspoon salt
2 tablespoons soy sauce
1/4 cup peanut oil
6 eggs, beaten until slightly frothy
1/2 cup (additional) soy sauce
1/2 cup cider vinegar
1/4 cup granulated sugar
1 tablespoon pine nuts, finely chopped (optional)

Mix the ground round steak, onion and garlic together. Set aside.

Place the sesame seed in a skillet over moderate heat. When the seeds begin to turn a golden brown and swell up, remove from the heat. Place the browned seeds in a bowl along with the salt and crush them with the back of a tablespoon. Add the crushed seeds, salt and 2 tablespoons of soy sauce to the meat mixture; mix well. Form the meat into 1/2-inch diameter meat balls.

Place 1 tablespoon of the oil in a large skillet over moderate heat and sauté the meatballs. Shake the pan back and forth so that the meatballs retain their round shape and are evenly browned.

Place another tablespoon of the oil in another large skillet or pancake griddle over moderate heat. Place 1 tablespoon of the eggs on the heated surface and allow it to spread out in a circle about 2-1/2 inches in diameter. As soon as the edges become firm, place a meatball on one half the circle. Using a spatula, turn the other half of the egg circle over the meatball. Press the edges slightly so that the runny portion of the circle completely seals the meatball inside. Continue to sauté for a few seconds longer until the omelets are firm and golden brown. Place the omelets on an oven-proof platter in a 250° F. oven until you have used up all of the egg and meatballs.

Mix the additional soy sauce, vinegar and sugar together. Place in 6 individual little dishes. Sprinkle the top with a bit of the chopped pine nuts. Serve as a dip with the little omelets. *Serves 6.*

SHRIMP AND EGG CAKES

6 eggs, beaten until frothy
1/4 teaspoon salt
1/2 teaspoon Accent
2 tablespoons soy sauce
1 cup green onion, thinly sliced; include a little of the green
1/4 cup celery, thinly sliced
1 4-ounce can mushroom stems and pieces, coarsely chopped
1 7-1/2-ounce can shrimp bits and pieces or 3/4 cup chopped
    shrimp
2 tablespoons peanut oil

Sauce:
1 10-ounce can chicken broth
1 tablespoon soy sauce
1/4 teaspoon granulated sugar
1/2 teaspoon (additional) Accent
2 tablespoons cornstarch

Mix the beaten eggs, salt, Accent, soy sauce, sliced green onion, celery, mushrooms and shrimp together well and set aside for 15 minutes to let the various flavors become united.

Heat the peanut oil over moderate heat in a large skillet or on a griddle. Drop tablespoonfuls of the egg mixture into the hot oil; allow them to form into lacy pancakes. Stir the egg mixture frequently so that the egg and solid ingredients are evenly mixed in each spoonful. Continue to cook the shrimp pancakes over moderate heat until the egg portions just begin to turn a golden brown and the tops are firm. Remove with a spatula and place on a heated platter in a 250°F. oven while you make the sauce.

Mix the chicken broth, soy sauce, sugar, Accent and cornstarch together well. Place over low heat and cook, stirring constantly, until glazed and thickened. Pour the hot sauce over the egg pancakes and serve at once. Serve 6.

BLEU CHEESE SQUARES

1 pkg bleu cheese salad dressing mix
2 T onion, grated
2 T butter
1 egg
1 pkg (8 oz) cream cheese
2 C flour
1 tsp salt
3/4 C shortening
6 T cold water

In a small bowl combine salad dressing mix, grated onion, butter, egg and cream cheese. Beat until thoroughly blended. Reserve. In separate bowl sift flour and salt. Cut in shortening until particles are fine. Add cold water, and stir with a fork until dough holds together. Roll out on floured board into a 14 x 20-inch rectangle. Cut into two 10 x 14-inch pieces. Spread cheese filling over one half. Top with other half and cut into 2-inch squares. Bake in 425°F. oven for 12 minutes or until lightly browned. Serve hot.

Makes 35 pieces.

HAM AND CHUTNEY SPREAD

1/2 C cooked ham, minced
1/2 C chutney, minced

Combine ingredients and mix well. Spread on crackers, wheat squares, or bread squares. May also be used to fill celery stalks into 1-1/2-inch lengths.

Makes approximately 1 cup.

SALMON SPREAD

1 C salmon, flaked
1/2 C mayonnaise
2 T onion, grated
1 tsp lemon juice

Combine all ingredients and mix well. Spread on your favorite crackers. Fresh vegetables such as celery cut into 1-inch lengths, carrot sticks, mushrooms or cauliflowerettes may also be used.

Makes approximately 1-1/2 cups.

GOLDEN CHEESE ROLLS

1 pkg pie crust mix
2 T sweet Vermouth
1-1/2 C Cheddar cheese, shredded
Paprika

Prepare pie crust mix as directed on package using 2 T Vermouth in place of part of the water. Divide dough in half. Roll each half on floured surface to a 12 x 4-inch rectangle. Sprinkle with cheese. Fold long edges over center, sealing edges and ends. Place seam side down on ungreased cookie sheet. Using sharp knife, cut halfway through rolls at 1-inch intervals. Sprinkle with paprika. Bake at 400° F. for 20 minutes, or until golden brown. Serve hot.

Makes about 24 pieces.

BAKED CLAMS ITALIANO

1 can (10-1/2 oz) minced clams
2 T olive oil
1 T grated onion
1 T minced parsley
1/8 tsp oregano
1/4 C *plus* 2 T bread crumbs
1 tsp garlic salt
2 T grated Parmesan cheese

Drain clams and reserve 3 T broth. Heat olive oil in small frying pan. onion, parsley, oregano and 1/4 cup bread crumbs for 2 minutes, or until onion is golden. Remove from heat and mix with clams, 3 T broth, and garlic salt. Spoon into a dozen clam or aluminum shells. Sprinkle lightly with a mixture made of 2 T bread crumbs and 2 T Parmesan cheese. Place on baking sheet and bake in 375°F. oven for 25 minutes, or until crusty on top.

Serves 6.

OLIVE SPREAD

1/2 C butter, softened
2 T milk
2 drops red food coloring
3 T stuffed green olives, chopped

In a small mixing bowl beat the butter, milk, and food coloring. Beat until fluffy. Stir in the olives. Spread on crackers. For variations, use yellow or green food coloring and arrange on serving tray.

Makes approximately 3/4 cup.

VEGETABLE HORS D'OEUVRES

1 pkg (3 oz) cream cheese
2 T milk
1/2 tsp curry powder
12 3-inch lengths celery
2 T dill, minced
18 cherry tomatoes
1/4 C mayonnaise
3 T chives, minced
2 medium-sized cucumbers
1 can (2 oz) deviled ham
2 T parsley, minced
12 mushroom caps
2 T butter

Soften cream cheese and mix with milk. Divide in half. Add curry powder to half of cream cheese mixture and use to stuff celery pieces. Add dill to remaining half of cream cheese and reserve. Hollow out cherry tomatoes and fill with mixture of mayonnaise and minced chives. Peel cucumbers and slice off each end. Using a sharp knife, remove seeds, making cucumbers into hollow tubes. Stuff with mixture of deviled ham and parsley. Refrigerate for 1 hour. Cut into 1/2-inch slices. Sauté mushroom caps in melted butter. Set aside. Chop stems fine and sauté. Mix with dill cream cheese mixture. Stuff mushroom caps. Refrigerate all until time to serve.

Serves 6.

EGG YOLK PANCAKES

4 egg yolks
1 tablespoon sugar
1/2 teaspoon salt
1 tablespoon melted butter
2 cups half-and-half cream
1-1/4 cups all-purpose flour
1 teaspoon baking powder

Beat the egg yolks until they are light and lemon colored. Gradually add the sugar, salt, melted butter and 1 cup of the half-and-half cream. Continue to beat until smooth.

Sift the flour and baking powder together twice; gradually add to the egg mixture, beating after each addition of flour. When you have added the rest of the flour, add the remaining cup of cream and mix well.

Bake on a lightly greased hot griddle; serve with syrup or fresh fruit. Makes 12 large pancakes. Serves 6, allowing 2 pancakes per person.

OATMEAL PANCAKES

1-1/2 cups "quick" rolled oats.
2 cups buttermilk
1/2 cup all-purpose flour
1 teaspoon sugar
1 teaspoon baking soda
2 eggs, separated

Mix the rolled oats with the buttermilk and allow to stand for 15 minutes.

Gradually beat in the flour, sugar and baking soda. Beat the mixture well after each addition.

Beat the egg yolks until they are light and lemon colored and then add to the buttermilk and oat mixture. Mix well.

Beat the egg whites until they stand in peaks. Fold the whites into the mixture, taking care not to lose any of the air.

Bake the pancakes on a hot, lightly greased griddle. Makes 1 dozen large pancakes. Serves 6, allowing 2 pancakes per person. These are delicious served with butter and brown sugar or with maple syrup.

EGG PANCAKES WITH SOUR CREAM

3 eggs
1/2 cup sour cream
1 cup buttermilk
1/2 teaspoon baking soda
1/2 teaspoon salt
1 tablespoon granulated sugar
1-1/2 cups all-purpose flour
2 teaspoons double action baking powder

Beat the eggs with a rotary or electric beater until they are well mixed and frothy. While still beating, add the sour cream and 1/2 cup of the buttermilk. Continue to beat until the mixture is bubbly.

Mix the soda, salt, sugar, flour and baking powder together and sift twice. Gradually add them to the egg and buttermilk mixture, beating after each addition. Then, add the remaining 1/2 cup of buttermilk.

Bake in large-sized pancakes on a hot, lightly greased griddle. Makes 1 dozen good-sized pancakes. Serves 6, allowing 2 pancakes per person.

RAW POTATO PANCAKES WITH EGGS

3 eggs, separated
2 3-inch diameter raw potatoes, scrubbed, but not peeled; grated
1/2 teaspoon salt
1 tablespoon granulated sugar
2 tablespoons all-purpose flour
1/2 teaspoon baking powder

Beat the egg yolks until light and lemon colored. Add the grated potatoes, salt, sugar, flour and baking powder. Mix all thoroughly.

Beat the egg whites until they stand in peaks; fold the beaten whites into the potato mixture taking care not to lose the air.

Fry on a lightly greased griddle in 3-inch diameter pancakes. Makes 1 dozen pancakes. Serve with applesauce and country sausages.

OYSTERS ST. JACQUES

6 hard-cooked eggs, peeled and coarsely chopped
1 quart stewing-size oysters and their liquid
1 bay leaf
1/2 teaspoon salt
1/4 teaspoon pepper
1/8 teaspoon thyme
3 tablespoons butter
1/4 cup green onion, finely chopped
1 tablespoon green pepper, finely chopped
3 tablespoons flour
1 tablespoon parsley, finely chopped
1 teaspoon Worcestershire sauce
1/2 cup half-and-half cream
1/2 cup (additional) butter
3/4 cup bread crumbs

Drain the oysters and measure the liquid. Add enough water to make 1 cup. Place in a saucepan with the bay leaf, salt, pepper and thyme. Cook over low heat until the liquid begins to simmer.

Melt the butter in a 2-quart saucepan. Add the onion and green pepper and cook over low heat until the onion begins to get transparent. Stir in the flour and continue to cook over low heat until it is bubbly. Add the hot oyster liquid. Mix well and continue to cook over low heat, stirring constantly, for 5 minutes longer.

Remove the bay leaf and discard. Add the oysters, parsley and Worcestershire sauce; cook and stir gently for 3 minutes longer. Remove from the heat, and add two tablespoons of the hot liquid to the half-and-half cream; then add the half-and-half cream to the oysters and liquid. Add the chopped hard-cooked eggs and mix so that they are evenly distributed. Divide into 6 portions and place in 6 individual, buttered casserole dishes.

Melt the half cup of butter in a skillet and add the bread crumbs. Toss the crumbs back and forth until all of them are evenly buttered. Sprinkle the buttered crumbs over the top of each casserole. Place the casseroles in a 350°F. oven for 10 minutes or until the bread crumbs are a delicate golden brown. Serve 6.

OYSTERS A LA POULETTE

1 quart oysters and their liquid
3 tablespoons butter
3 tablespoons all-purpose flour
1/4 cup green onion, finely chopped
1 tablespoon parsley, finely chopped
1-1/2 cups half-and-half cream
4 egg yolks, beaten until lemon yellow
1/4 teaspoon grated lemon rind
2 tablespoons lemon juice
1/2 teaspoon salt
1/4 teaspoon freshly ground pepper
3 drops Tobasco sauce
1/2 cup (additional) butter
1 cup bread crumbs

Drain the oysters and reserve their liquid.

Melt the butter in a 1-quart saucepan; blend in the flour. Cook over low heat until the flour and butter begin to bubble. Add the chopped onion and the parsley. Continue to cook over low heat for 3 minutes or until the onion becomes slightly transparent. Add the liquid from the oysters, and continue to cook over very low heat, stirring constantly, for 8 minutes longer. Remove from the heat.

Mix the half-and-half cream with the beaten yolks; add to the oyster liquid and onion mixture. Stir until smoothly blended. Add the oysters and cook over low heat, stirring constantly, for 5 minutes longer. Add the lemon rind, lemon juice, salt, pepper and Tobasco sauce. Mix all well. Pour into six individual casserole dishes.

Melt the additional half cup of butter in a skillet over low heat. Add the bread crumbs and mix until all are evenly buttered. Place a portion of the buttered bread crumbs over the top of each casserole.

Place the casseroles in a 350° F. oven for 20 minutes or until the crumbs are a rich golden brown. Serves 6.

MARINATED OLIVES SAN ANTONIO

2 cans (5-1/4 oz) pitted ripe olives
2 garlic cloves, minced
2 T minced onion
2 T wine vinegar
3 T olive oil
1/4 tsp salt
Pepper to taste

Drain olives. Place olives in a large jar with screw top. Add other ingredients. Close tightly. Shake jar vigorously. Refrigerate at least overnight. Shake jar several times during refrigeration. These olives will keep in the refrigerator for a week.

CLAM DIP

1 can (7 oz) minced clams
1 pkg (8 oz) cream cheese, softened
1-1/2 tsp Worcestershire sauce
1/2 tsp garlic salt
2 tsp lemon juice
1 tsp onion juice

Drain broth from minced clams and reserve. Mash cream cheese until soft. Combine with all other ingredients except clam juice. Thin mixture to desired consistency with clam juice. Serve at room temperature. Use your favorite item to dip with.

Makes approximately 1-1/2 - 2 cups.

ZINGY AVOCADO DIP

1-1/2 C celery, diced
1 avocado, peeled and diced
1 C French dressing
1 T prepared horseradish
1 pkg (8 oz) cream cheese, softened
1/3 C sour cream
1 T onion powder
1 tsp garlic salt

Combine all ingredients in blender. Serve with raw vegetables, assorted crackers, or potato chips. May also be served spread on crackers, or celery if desired.

Makes approximately 3-1/2 cups.

PARTY MIX

1 stick margarine
1 T Worcestershire sauce
1 T garlic salt
2 C wheat square cereal
2 C corn square cereal
2 C rice square cereal
1 can (7-1/2 oz) salted peanuts
2 C thin pretzel sticks, broken

Heat oven to 250° F. Melt margarine in a large shallow baking dish. Mix in Worcestershire sauce and garlic salt. Add cereals, peanuts and pretzels and mix thoroughly. Bake in oven for one hour, stirring every 15 minutes. Cool and store in airtight container.

Makes about 2 quarts

DEVILED HAM AND EGG SPREAD

1 can (4-1/2 oz) deviled ham
1 egg, hard cooked and chopped
1 T mayonnaise
1 T chili sauce
1/2 tsp mustard

Combine all ingredients and mix well. Add more mayonnaise if necessary for easy spreading. Spread on your favorite crackers, bread squares, or toast thins.

Makes approximately 1 cup.

LIPTAUER CHEESE

1 pkg (8 oz) cream cheese, softened
8 oz cottage cheese
1/2 lb butter, softened
3 T paprika
4 tsp grated onion
4 tsp minced parsley
1 tsp garlic salt
1/4 C sour cream

Combine all ingredients in a mixing bowl. Stir until thoroughly blended. Cover and refrigerate until serving time. Serve with assorted crackers or raw vegetables such as celery sticks, carrot sticks or cauliflowerettes.

Makes approximately 3-1/2 cups.

SESAME TARTS

2 T sesame seeds
1 pkg pie crust mix

Combine sesame seeds with pie crust mix. Follow directions on package to make pie crust pastry. Chill for 10 minutes. Roll out to 1/4-inch thickness. Cut into 2-inch rounds, preferably scalloped. Place each round into a small muffin tin, and bake at 400° F. for 15 minutes, or until golden brown. Cool and fill tarts with your favorite filling, spread, or dip.

Makes about 35.

TAMPA BLACK BEAN DIP

1 can (10-1/2 oz) black bean soup
1 medium onion, chopped
1 pkg (8 oz) cream cheese
1 T milk
1/2 tsp garlic salt
1 tsp Worchestershire sauce
2 tsp parsley, minced

Combine all ingredients except parsley in blender. Blend just until smooth. Add more milk if desired to thin mixture. Spoon into serving dish and garnish with parsley. Serve with assorted crackers, pretzels, chips or raw vegetables.

Makes approximately 2 cups.

VITELLO TONATO

4 C water
1 C dry white wine
1 onion, quartered
2 cloves
2 stalks celery, cut into 1-inch pieces
2 carrots, cut into 1-inch pieces
4 T chopped parsley
1 tsp salt
1/2 tsp pepper
1 2-lb boned leg of veal, rolled and tied

In a deep heavy pan combine the water, wine, onion, cloves, celery, carrots, parsley, salt and pepper. Bring to a slow boil and add the veal. Add hot water if necessary to cover the veal. When water reaches a boil again, cover and simmer for 1-1/2 hours. Remove from broth, cool to room temperature and refrigerate. Strain broth and save to use as stock in gravies, soups, etc.

1 can (7 oz) white meat tuna fish, drained
4 flat anchovy fillets
1/4 C olive oil
1/4 C vegetable oil
6 T lemon juice
6 stuffed green olives, sliced in half

Process tuna, anchovy fillets, oils, and lemon juice in blender until smooth. Slice the cooled veal very thin and arrange on a serving dish. Pour sauce over the veal and refrigerate. Just before serving, garnish with the sliced olives.

Serves 8.

APPLE GLAZED HAM LOAF

HAM LOAF:

2 lbs lean pork, ground
1 lb ham, ground
1 medium onion, chopped
1/2 C celery, chopped
2 eggs
1/2 C evaporated milk
1/4 tsp black pepper
1/2 C dry bread crumbs

Mix all ham loaf ingredients well and form into a loaf. Place in roasting pan and bake in 350°F. oven for 1 hour. Remove from oven.

GLAZE TOPPING:

1/2 C apple juice
1 tsp cornstarch
1/4 tsp allspice
2 T brown sugar
1 large firm apple

In a small saucepan combine apple juice, cornstarch, allspice and sugar. Heat and stir until sugar melts and mixture thickens slightly. Core and slice the apple. Arrange slices on top of the ham loaf. Pour glaze over the apples and ham loaf and bake an additional half hour in 350°F. oven. Cool thoroughly before serving.

Serves 8.

MAIN DISHES

FESTIVE MEAT LOAF

Here is a meat loaf made with, of all things, fruit. There is a festive air about it, and an outstandingly different flavor.

1-1/2 pounds hamburger
1 pound lean ground pork
1 teaspoon salt
1/4 teaspoon pepper
2 eggs
1 teaspoon monosodium glutamate
4 cups soft bread crumbs

Filling

3/4 cup seedless raisins
1/4 cup dried apricots, cut into 1/8" slices
1/2 cup chopped onion
1/4 cup chopped parsley
1/4 teaspoon sage
1/4 teaspoon thyme
1/2 cup water or bouillon

Mix the meat, salt, pepper, eggs, monosodium glutamate and bread crumbs thoroughly. Spread on a sheet of aluminum foil, forming a rectangle about 1/2" thick.

Mix the ingredients of the filling and spread evenly over the meat mixture. Now, carefully roll up the meat as you would a jelly roll. Bring up the top and bottom edges of the foil and fold them together tightly; the sides of the foil should be folded over to keep in the juices and the flavor.

Place the foil-wrapped roll on a flat tin in a 350° F. preheated oven for 1-1/2 hours. At the end of the first hour, open the foil and spread away from the sides of the loaf to allow browning.

SIMPLE MEAT LOAF

1-1/2 pounds hamburger
1/2 pound lean ground pork
1/4 cup chopped onion
1/8 teaspoon pepper
1 medium carrot, grated*
1 medium raw potato, grated
2 eggs, beaten until lemon yellow
3/4 cup condensed milk or rich milk from the top of the bottle
2 cups bread crumbs

Mix all of the ingredients in the order in which they are listed. Stir thoroughly. Press into a greased loaf tin and bake in a preheated 350°F. oven for 1 hour.

When serving, garnish with chopped parsley.

*If you have leftover cooked carrots or potatoes, these may be used instead of the raw ones.

MEAT LOAF WITH MUSHROOM SOUP

4 slices white bread with crusts removed
2 eggs, beaten to a lemon yellow
1-1/2 pounds hamburger
1/4 teaspoon salt
1/4 teaspoon pepper
1 can condensed cream of mushroom soup
1/2 cup dried mushrooms (optional, but very nice to add)

Crumble the bread into the beaten eggs, then mix in all the rest of the ingredients in the order listed above. Spoon gently into a greased loaf tin. Place in a preheated 350°F. oven for 1 hour.

Fresh mushrooms, quartered, may be used in this recipe instead of the dried ones. If you are using the fresh ones, sauté a few to be used for a garnish around the edges of the plate when serving.

CHEESE AND TOMATO OMELET

Omelet:
6 eggs, separated
2 tablespoons milk
1/2 teaspoon salt
1/4 teaspoon pepper
2 tablespoons butter

Topping:
1 #2 can stewed tomatoes (most supermarkets carry these
   tomatoes already stewed with green pepper, etc.)
1 tablespoon butter
1/2 teaspoon salt
1/8 teaspoon pepper
1 teaspoon granulated sugar
1 cup grated American cheese

Beat the egg yolks until they are light and lemon colored; add
the milk, salt and pepper. Mix well. Beat the egg whites until
they stand in stiff peaks. Fold the beaten whites into the egg yolk
mixture. Melt the butter in a 10-inch skillet over moderate heat;
swirl the butter around so that it covers the sides of the pan as
well as the bottom. Pour in the egg mixture and continue to
cook over moderate heat for 7 minutes or until the omelet has
set.

Place the tomatoes, butter, salt, pepper and sugar in a
saucepan and place over moderate heat. Cook for 10 minutes or
until slightly thickened.

Using a spatula, lift the omelet around the edges from time to
time to loosen it from the bottom of the pan. When the bottom
of the omelet is a golden brown, place half the tomatoes over the
surface. Follow this with all the grated cheese. Place the omelet,
still in the skillet, in a 350° F. oven for about 10 minutes or until
the cheese has melted.

Remove the omelet from the oven and fold in half. Slide the
folded omelet on to a heated serving platter and drizzle the
remainder of the tomatoes over the top for garnish.

Serve piping hot. Serves 6.

A SUNDAY NIGHT OMELET

1/3 cup butter
1/3 cup flour
1-1/2 cups milk
1/2 teaspoon salt
1/2 teaspoon Accent
2 7-1/2-ounce cans tiny shrimp, drained
6 eggs, separated
1/4 (additional) cup butter
2 tablespoons parsley, finely chopped

Melt the 1/3 cup butter in the top of a double boiler; stir in the flour until it is smoothly blended. Add the milk, salt and Accent and place over boiling water. Cook, stirring constantly, until the mixture has thickened. Remove 2/3 cup of the thickened sauce and set aside to cool to room temperature. Add the drained shrimp to the remainder of the cream sauce in the double boiler. Cover and turn the heat back to barely simmering.

Beat the egg yolks until light colored and slightly thickened; add the cooled white sauce and beat again to mix thoroughly.

Beat the egg whites until they are stiff and stand in peaks. Fold the beaten egg whites into the yolk-cream sauce mixture.

Melt the additional butter in a 10-inch skillet with a fitted cover. Pour the egg mixture into the skillet. Smooth the top slightly with a rubber spoon. Lightly butter the skillet's cover and place over the omelet. Cook on top of the stove over low heat for 15 minutes or until the sides and the bottom of the omelet have turned a light golden brown and the omelet is puffed up and cooked through.

Cut through the center with a sharp knife to within 1/2 inch of the bottom. Loosen the omelet and transfer to a heated platter. Pour the heated shrimp mixture over half the omelet and then fold the other half over the top of the shrimp. Garnish the top with a sprinkle of parsley. Serve at once. Serves 4.

HAMBURGER PANCAKE LOAF

This is a recipe from the Ukraine region of Russia. When I first heard of it, it seemed impossible that you could make meat loaf with pancakes; but you can, and it is delicious.

1 cup flour
1/2 teaspoon salt
1/2 teaspoon baking powder
2 raw eggs
1 cup milk
1 tablespoon butter or margarine
1 pound ground chuck
1 small onion, minced
1/4 teaspoon salt
1/2 teaspoon pepper
1/2 teaspoon Accent
2 hard-boiled eggs, chopped
1/4 cup stock, or 1/4 cup water with 1 bouillon cube dissolved
 in it
1/4 cup buttered browned bread crumbs

Place the flour in a bowl and mix in the 1/2 teaspoon salt and the baking powder. Beat the raw eggs in the milk. Slowly stir the egg and milk mixture into the flour. Stir very well, then set aside for 25 minutes.

Meanwhile, melt the butter in a skillet, then place the ground meat in the skillet and fry until golden brown. Add the onion, 1/4 teaspoon salt, pepper and Accent. Remove from heat and add the chopped hard-boiled eggs, then the stock. Stir, mixing all well.

Heat a griddle and place 1 tablespoon of batter for each of the pancakes on it. Brown on both sides; set the finished pancakes aside until all the batter is used up.

Place pancakes to cover the bottom of a greased loaf tin. Follow with about a half-inch layer of the meat mixture. Continue alternate layers of pancakes and meat until all is used up. You should end with pancakes on the last layer. Sprinkle the bread crumbs over all. Bake in a 350°F. oven for 20 minutes.

CHICK PEA-HAMBURGER LOAF

1 cup dried chick peas*
5 strips bacon, cut into 1/4" cubes
2 medium onions, diced
1 pound ground beef
1/4 teaspoon grated nutmeg
1/2 teaspoon Accent
1/4 teaspoon grated lemon rind
1/2 teaspoon salt
1/4 teaspoon pepper
Juice of 1 lemon
1/2 cup catsup
3/4 cup precooked rice
1/2 cup stock, or 2 bouillon cubes dissolved in 1/2 cup water.

After having soaked the chick peas for at least 6 hours, drain them and cover with cold water. Bring them to a boil, then lower the heat and cook for at least 30 minutes, or until they can be pierced with a sharp fork. Drain and set aside to cool.

Fry the cubed bacon until it is brown and crisp. Remove bacon with a slotted spoon and set aside until later; reserve half of the bacon drippings in the skillet. Fry the onions in the bacon fat until they are glazed and transparent. Now fry the ground beef until it loses its red color. Add the grated nutmeg, Accent, lemon rind, salt and pepper. Continue to cook for 5 minutes longer and then add the lemon juice and catsup. Stir in the rice just as it comes from the package, and then add the stock.

Arrange half of the chick peas on the bottom of a greased loaf pan. Over this place the hamburger mixture. Arrange the remainder of the chick peas on top. Pour the stock over it, and place in a 350° F. oven for 35 minutes. Turn loaf onto a heated platter and sprinkle bacon cubes over the top.

*If your local grocer does not have them, they can be purchased in an international food store or one specializing in Greek, Armenian or Turkish food.

RUSSIAN MEAT LOAF

1 cup rice
2 cups water
3 hard-boiled eggs
1 medium-sized onion, chopped fine
1 tablespoon butter
3 slices white bread, broken into coarse crumbs and moistened
   in 1/4 cup water
1 pound hamburger
1/2 teaspoon monosodium glutamate
1/2 teaspoon salt
1/4 teaspoon pepper

Boil the rice in the water for 15 minuts in a covered pan. At the end of this time the grains should be fluffy and tender. Rinse in warm water and drain thoroughly. Chop the hard-boiled eggs into coarse pieces so that they keep their yellow and white identity. Fold the eggs into the boiled rice. In a small pan, sauté the onion in the butter until it is transparent but not brown.

Mix the sautéed onion and the moistened bread crumbs with the hamburger. Add the monosodium glutamate, salt and pepper. Flatten the meat mixture on a piece of aluminum foil, making a circle about the size of a pie plate.

Place the rice and egg mixture in the middle of the meat circle. Using the foil for support, bring up the sides of the meat until the rice and egg mixture is completely hidden. Leave a small opening in the top of the foil for the steam to escape.

Place in a flat pan and bake in a preheated 350°F. oven for 45 minutes. Garnish with chopped parsley if you want additional color.

FRENCH MEAT LOAF WITH LEEK

Leek is an unusual vegetable which few but the French know how to use. If you want a meat loaf that is both different and delightful in flavor, try this one.

2 eggs, beaten to a lemon-yellow color
1/2 cup water
4 slices white bread with the crusts removed
1/2 cup chopped onion
1 can tomato soup
1 pound hamburger
1/2 teaspoon salt
1/4 teaspoon pepper
1/8 teaspoon nutmeg
2 good-sized leeks

Beat the eggs, then add the water. Break up the bread and add to the egg-and-water mixture. Add the onion and 1/4 of the can of tomato soup. Reserve the remainder of the soup until later. Add the meat to the softened bread mixture, along with the salt, pepper and nutmeg. Mix all very thoroughly and set aside.

Thoroughly butter the sides and bottom of a loaf tin. Wash the leeks and remove the harsh outer leaves. Cut into 1/8" slices. Line the bottom of the buttered loaf tin with slices of leek, reserving the rest of the slices until later.

Gently spoon the meat mixture into the loaf pan over the leek. Pour over the meat mixture the remainder of the tomato soup. Arrange the rest of the leek over the top. Place in a preheated 350°F. oven and bake for 1 hour.

This loaf is excellent served with plain boiled potatoes.

MACARONI SOUFFLE WITH CREAMED TUNA

1 6-ounce package elbow macaroni
1/4 cup butter
1/4 cup flour
1 teaspoon salt
1/8 teaspoon pepper
1-1/4 cups milk
5 eggs, separated
2 10-ounce cans cream of chicken soup
2 7-1/2-ounce cans light meat tuna fish, drained well

Boil the macaroni until tender according to package directions. Drain and set aside.

Melt the butter in a saucepan over moderate heat. Stir in the flour, salt and pepper and mix until smooth and free of lumps. Add the milk and continue to cook over moderate heat, stirring constantly, until the sauce is thickened and creamy. Remove from the heat and allow to cool to room temperature.

Beat the egg yolks until light and slightly thickened. Beat 1/2 cup of the thickened, cooled cream sauce into the egg yolks; then add the remainder of the cream sauce to the yolks, beating until all is well mixed.

Stir the drained macaroni into the egg yolk mixture and mix well.

Beat the egg whites until they stand in peaks and are shiny, but not dry. Gently fold the egg whites into the macaroni and egg yolk mixture.

Line a well-greased ring mold with white bakery paper cut to fit the sides, bottom and the ring opening. The paper may overlap if necessary to cover all of the metal of the ring mold. Butter the paper lining with a little melted butter and a pastry brush. Using a rubber spoon, carefully place the egg and macaroni mixture around the sides of the mold. Place in a 325°F. oven for 45 minutes or until a table knife inserted into the middle of the mixture comes out clean.

While the ring is baking, place the two cans of cream of chicken soup over barely boiling water in the top of a double boiler. Flake the drained tuna fish and add to the cream of chicken soup. Cover and allow to heat through.

When the macaroni-soufflé ring is done, unmold on a heated platter and pour the creamed tuna mixture into the middle. Serve at once, piping hot. Serves 6.

ORANGE DESSERT SOUFFLE

Soufflé:
1/3 cup soft butter
1/3 cup all-purpose flour
1/8 teaspoon salt
1 cup milk
1/2 cup thawed frozen orange juice concentrate
6 eggs, separated
1/4 cup granulated sugar

Topping:
1 8-ounce can mandarin oranges
1/2 cup granulated sugar
2 tablespoons cornstarch
1/2 cup thawed frozen orange juice concentrate

Melt the butter in a saucepan; stir in the flour and salt and cook until the mixture begins to bubble. Add the milk and cook over low heat, stirring constantly, until the mixture is thick. Remove from the heat and add the thawed orange juice concentrate. Mix well and set aside to cool slightly.

Beat the egg yolks until they are thick and lemon colored; add 3 tablespoons of the orange-flavored mixture and mix well. Then add the egg yolks to the orange mixture and stir until thoroughly mixed.

Beat the egg whites until they just begin to stand in peaks; gradually add the sugar and continue to beat until they stand in glossy peaks. Carefully fold the egg whites into the yolk-orange mixture. Pour into a suitable unbuttered casserole dish. Bake in a 300°F. oven for 1-1/4 hours or until a table knife inserted in the middle comes out clean.

For the topping, drain the mandarin oranges, reserving the juice. Add enough water to the juice to make 1 cup. Mix the sugar and cornstarch together thoroughly; stir into the juice and water and mix until smooth. Place in a saucepan over low heat and add the thawed orange juice concentrate. Cook over low heat, stirring constantly, until the mixture becomes thickened. Remove from heat and stir in the mandarin orange sections. Take care not to break up the orange sections. Serve warm over portions of the soufflé. Serves 6.

WHEATIES MEAT LOAF
WITH VEGETABLE SOUP

1-1/2 pounds hamburger
1/4 cup chopped onion
1/2 teaspoon salt
1/4 teaspoon ground pepper
1/2 teaspoon Accent
2 cups Wheaties cereal
1 egg, beaten with 1 tablespoon water
1 can beef-vegetable soup

Mix all ingredients with the exception of the soup. Stir until all are well blended. Finally, fold in the soup, taking care that you do not mash the vegetables beyond identification.

Put into a greased loaf pan and bake in a preheated 350°F. oven for 1 hour, or until center of loaf is firm to the touch. Baste from time to time with the liquid which gathers around the loaf.

This loaf is very colorful when sliced. It is excellent served cold.

Variations:

Substitute 1 can cream of mushroom soup for the beef vegetable
   soup.
Substitute 1 can cream of chicken soup for the beef vegetable
   soup.
Substitute 1 can cream of celery soup for beef vegetable soup.
For a wonderful flavor, add 3 tablespoons wheat germ.
Substitute Cheerios for Wheaties.
Substitute 4 shredded wheat biscuits for Wheaties.
Substitute Rice Chex for Wheaties.

HAM-HAMBURGER MEAT LOAF

This is one of my favorite meat loaf recipes because it tastes so good in sandwiches. It blends well with either whole wheat or rye bread.

1-1/2 pounds hamburger
1 pound ground ham (we usually ask the butcher to save boiled
    ham ends to grind for this)
2 eggs, beaten until lemon yellow
1/2 cup condensed milk
1 cup soft bread crumbs
1/4 teaspoon pepper
1/4 teaspoon dry mustard
1 teaspoon Accent
1/8 teaspoon ground cloves
4 slices pineapple
1 tablespoon brown sugar

Mix very thoroughly all of the ingredients except the pineapple and brown sugar. Form into a loaf and place in a buttered loaf tin. If your family likes a crisp outside on a loaf, this one can be made in an oblong shape and baked on a flat coffee-cake tin.

Place the pineapple slices on the top and hold them in place with toothpicks. Sprinkle the brown sugar over each slice. Place loaf in a preheated 350°F. oven and bake for 1 hour, or until firm to the touch.

Leftover ham can be frozen successfully. The next time you bake a big ham, freeze the scraps to use in this recipe.

CHINESE CHOW MEIN LOAF

2 pounds hamburger
1 cup celery, cut into 1/4" pieces
1 cup onion, cut into 1/4" pieces
1 cup rice
1 can cream of mushroom soup
1 can cream of celery soup
1/4 cup milk
1/2 teaspoon salt
1/4 teaspoon pepper
1 #2 can chow mein noodles.

Brown the hamburger in a deep skillet until it is all separated. Add the celery and onion. Cook over low heat until the onion is transparent and glazed. Meanwhile, place the rice in two cups of water and cook for 15 minutes, or until fluffy and tender. Rinse the rice in warm water, drain and add to the hamburger mixture.

Stir in the mushroom soup and celery soup. Add the milk, salt and pepper. Mix all very thoroughly. Put into a greased 1-1/2 quart casserole; sprinkle the chow mein noodles over the top. Place in a 350° F. oven for 30 minutes. Serve with soy sauce if desired.

VEAL LOAF

2-1/2 cups moist bread crumbs
3 eggs, beaten until lemon yellow
2 tablespoons grated onion
Juice of 1 lemon
2 teaspoons salt
1/2 teaspoon pepper
2 pounds ground veal
1/4 pound salt pork, ground with the veal
1/2 cup cracker crumbs
4 strips salt pork

Add the bread crumbs to the beaten eggs; stir in the grated onion and the lemon juice. Add the salt and pepper. Mix in the ground veal and pork. Stir all very well.

Shape into an oblong loaf and place on a sheet of heavy aluminum foil. Press the cracker crumbs into the sides and over the top. Place the strips of salt pork diagonally across the loaf. Fold up the sides of the aluminum foil to retain the juices. Bake in a preheated 425° F. oven for 30 minutes. Then reduce heat to 300° F. and bake for an additional 1 hour and 30 minutes.

SELF-GLAZING MEAT LOAF

1 cup V-8 vegetable juice cocktail
3 slices bread, fresh and soft
3 eggs
1 teaspoon salt
1/4 teaspoon pepper
1 tablespoon minced onion
1 pound ground chuck
1/2 pound ground ham
1/2 pound ground veal
4 tablespoons dark brown sugar
4 tablespoons cider vinegar
1/4 teaspoon dry mustard
Dash of cayenne
2 tablespoons Worcestershire sauce
2 tablespoons water

Put the V-8 juice into a small saucepan and heat thoroughly. Place the bread, well broken up, into a medium-sized mixing bowl. Pour the vegetable cocktail over it. With the beaters of your mixer at low speed, beat until the bread and juice are thoroughly mixed and cooled. Then turn your mixer to its highest speed and add the eggs, one at a time. Add the salt, pepper and onion.

Now stir in the ground meat by hand. Be sure that all is thoroughly mixed. Mix the sugar, vinegar, dry mustard, cayenne, Worcestershire sauce and water together. Pour this into the bottom of a loaf tin. Form the meat mixture into a loaf and place in the tin. Bake in a 375° F. oven for 1 hour. At the end of this time, invert the loaf on an ovenproof platter and continue to bake for 30 minutes longer. The glaze which was at the bottom of the loaf will now glaze the top. If you wish, spoon the glaze over the top and sides from time to time.

MEAT LOAF WITH APPLE SAUCE

1 pound lean ground beef
3/4 pound pork sausages (remove casings)
1/2 teaspoon sage
1 tablespoon Worcestershire sauce
1/2 teaspoon salt
2 cups canned apple sauce
1-1/2 cups very dry bread crumbs
4 twists of pepper mill

Mix all of the ingredients together in the order in which they are given. Butter a loaf tin and pack them into it. Bake in a 350°F. oven for 45 minutes. This delicious meat loaf is excellent served cold in sandwiches.

LIMA BEAN, RICE AND HAMBURGER LOAF
(a good stretcher recipe)

1 pound hamburger
1/2 teaspoon paprika
1/2 cup chopped onion
1/2 teaspoon salt
1/4 teaspoon pepper
1 tablespoon parsley flakes
1 cup rice
2 #2 cans lima beans, drained
1 cup stock, or 2 bouillon cubes dissolved in 1 cup water
1 can condensed tomato soup

Sauté the hamburger in a skillet until it loses is reddish color. Add the paprika and the chopped onion and continue to cook over low heat for 5 minutes longer. Then remove from heat.

Add the salt, pepper and parsley flakes; stir in the rice just as it comes from the package. Last, stir in the lima beans, stock and tomato soup. Take care not to break up the lima beans.

Place the mixture in a well-greased loaf tin and bake at 350°F, for 45 minutes, or until the center of the loaf is firm.

MEAT LOAF RING WITH CREAMED BEANS

1/2 pound ground veal
1/2 pound ground pork
1/2 pound ground ham
1/2 teaspoon salt
4 twists of pepper mill
2 eggs
4 tablespoons instant flour
2 tablespoons instant onion
1 can cream of mushroom soup
1/2 cup dry bread crumbs
1 package frozen green beans in cream sauce

Mix the ground veal, and ham together very well. Add the salt, pepper and eggs. Mix until all are thoroughly blended. Add the flour and the onion and stir again. Stir in the cream of mushroom soup. Grease a ring mold with butter and coat the inside with the bread crumbs. Carefully pour in the meat mixture; spread evenly with a rubber spatula.

Place in a 375°F. oven in a pan of water. Bake in the pan for 1 hour. Remove from oven and let cool for 5 minutes. Cook the green beans in a double boiler until they are thoroughly thawed and tender.

Invert the meat mold on a platter and pour the green beans into the center. Serve piping hot.

Variations:

Substitute 1 can cream of mushroom soup and 1 cup mushroom stems and pieces for the green beans.
Substitute 1 package frozen creamed peas for the green beans.
Substitute 1 package frozen cream-style corn for the green beans.
Substitute 1 can cream of celery soup plus 1 cup cooked celery for the green beans.
Substitute 1 package frozen peas and 1 can cream of celery soup for the green beans.

MEAT LOAF WITH YOGHURT

1 cup yoghurt
1 package onion soup mix
3 eggs, well beaten
1/4 teaspoon pepper
1 teaspoon salt
1 tablespoon butter or margarine
1 cup soft bread crumbs (do not use crusts)
1-1/2 pounds chopped beef

Mix the yoghurt, onion soup mix and eggs very well. Add the pepper and salt and set aside to allow the flavors to blend. Melt the butter or margarine in a large skillet. Add the chopped beef and brown evenly until all of the meat is well separated. Mix the bread crumbs with the eggs, yoghurt and onion soup.

Strain the browned meat through a sieve so that there is no fat left in it. Reserve the drippings. Add the browned meat to the other ingredients and mix very well. Use a small portion of the drippings to grease a loaf tin. Place the meat mixture in the tin and bake at 375° F. for 30 minutes, or until the center of the loaf is firm.

Invert the loaf on a hot platter and place under the broiler for 5 minutes to brown the bottom; then remove from oven.

FESTIVE MEAT LOAF #2

1 pound ground beef
1 pound ground veal
3 eggs, beaten to a lemon yellow
1/2 cup catsup
1 teaspoon salt
1/4 teaspoon pepper
1/2 cup onion, chopped very fine
1/2 cup green pepper, chopped very fine
1 cup cracker crumbs
1 can tomato soup
1/4 cup water

Mix the ground meat with the eggs, catsup, salt, pepper, onion and green pepper. Add the cracker crumbs and mix all very thoroughly. Place in a suitable loaf pan, cover tightly with aluminum foil and bake at 400° F. for 45 minutes. Then remove foil and pour the tomato soup, mixed with the water, over the loaf. Continue to bake for 15 minutes.

Invert on a heated platter and garnish with parsley sprigs. This will serve about 8.

CAULIFLOWER MEAT LOAF

1 large head cauliflower (approximately 8″ in diameter) or two
  small heads
4 strips bacon, diced into 1/4″ pieces
1 pound ground chuck
1/2 teaspoon salt
4 twists of pepper mill
2 tablespoons dehydrated onion
1 cup moist bread crumbs
3/4 cup milk
4 eggs, beaten until lemon yellow
Dash of paprika

Wash the cauliflower well and break it into pieces. If there is a
large core, cut it into slices. Place in cold water and bring to a
boil. When the larger stems can be pierced with a fork, remove
from heat and drain. Set aside to cool. Brown the diced bacon in
a frying pan. Remove bacon and set aside; then brown the
ground chuck in the bacon drippings. Add the salt, pepper and
dehydrated onion.

Cover the bottom of a greased loaf pan with pieces of
cauliflower. Sprinkle with some of the bread crumbs. Follow
this with a layer of the ground meat. Repeat until all of the
cauliflower, bread crumbs and meat are used up. Add the milk
to the eggs and mix very well. Pour this over the ingredients in
the loaf tin. Sprinkle bacon over the top.

Place in a 300° F. oven for 45 minutes, or until the egg mixture
has set like a custard. Invert on a hot platter and garnish with
paprika.

DEER HUNTER'S PIE

1 pound hamburger
4 large boiled potatoes, peeled and sliced 1/8″ thick
2 large onions, peeled and sliced 1/8″ thick
3 large apples, preferably tart baking variety, sliced 1/8″ thick
1 cup beef stock, or 1 cup water with 3 bouillon cubes dissolved
   in it
1/4 teaspoon grated nutmeg
1/4 teaspoon pepper
1/2 teaspoon salt
1/2 cup bread crumbs

Sauté the hamburger in a skillet until it is lightly browned and completely separated.

Arrange a layer of potatoes over the bottom of a 1-1/2 quart greased casserole, follow with a layer of meat, a layer of onions and a layer of apples. Repeat until you have used up all of the ingredients.

Heat the beef stock, add the nutmeg, pepper and salt. Stir well so that all of the salt is dissolved. Pour this over the casserole. Sprinkle the bread crumbs over the top, and add little dabs of butter if you like. Bake in a 350° F. oven for 50 minutes.

HAMBURGER OYSTER CASSEROLE

2-1/2 pounds hamburger
1 pint oysters (save the liquor)
1 cup dry bread crumbs
4 sprigs parsley, chopped fine
1 small onion, chopped very fine
1 teaspoon salt
1/4 teaspoon ground pepper

Fry the hamburger loosely until it is all browned, turning with a spatula during frying so that it is not broken up too much. Then add the drained oysters, and continue frying until the oyster edges curl—about 5 minutes. Set aside, and mix the liquor from the oysters with the bread crumbs, parsley and onion. Season with the salt and pepper. Add to the browned meat and oysters, tossing lightly to mix. Put into a well-greased casserole and bake at 350° F. for 45 minutes. Before removing from oven, slip under the broiler for a few seconds so the top can brown.

MEXICAN CASSEROLE

3/4 pound ground chuck
3/4 pound lean ground pork
2 cups cooked broad noodles
1 8-ounce can tomato sauce
2 cups American process cheese, diced into 1/4" pieces
1/4 cup minced parsley
3 preserved pimentos, sliced into long strips 1/4" wide
1 green pepper, diced into 1/4" pieces
2 cups onion, diced into 1/4" pieces
1/2 teaspoon paprika
1 teaspoon salt
4 twists of pepper mill
4 strips bacon, diced into 1/4" pieces

Mix together all of the ingredients except the diced bacon. Sprinkle the bacon over the bottom of a 1-1/2 quart buttered casserole. Top the bacon with the meat and vegetable mixture. Bake in a 350°F. oven for 1 hour.

HAMBURGER-CABBAGE CASSEROLE

1 pound hamburger
1 tablespoon dehydrated onion
4 eggs
1 cup of milk
1 teaspoon sugar
1/2 teaspoon salt
1/4 teaspoon pepper
1 2-pound cabbage
1/2 cup bread crumbs

Brown the hamburger and cook until it is all separated. Add the onion and cook for a few minutes longer. Remove from the heat. Beat the eggs until they are lemon yellow, add the milk gradually and continue beating. Add the sugar to the milk and eggs. Stir in the hamburger. Add the salt and pepper. Mix well.

Slice the cabbage very fine. Cover with water and cook for 7 minutes; drain, discarding the water. Place the boiled cabbage in a deep, greased casserole. Pour the hamburger mixture over the cabbage. Sprinkle the top with bread crumbs. Bake in a 350°F. oven for 50 minutes.

The bread crumbs should become golden brown during this cooking time. If they are not, place the casserole under the broiler for a few minutes before serving.

RAW POTATO CASSEROLE

1/2 pound ground chuck
1/2 pound lean ground pork
1 can condensed tomato soup
1/2 teaspoon salt
4 twists of pepper mill
1 tablespoon flour
2 tablespoons butter or margarine
1 8-ounce can mushroom stems and pieces (do not drain)
1 large onion, diced
3 cups raw potatoes, diced in 1/2" pieces

Mix the ground meat with the tomato soup, salt and pepper. Work in the flour. Form into meat balls about the size of golf balls. Melt the butter in a skillet and brown the meat balls on all sides.

Place the meat balls on the bottom of a well-greased 1-1/2-quart casserole. Mix the mushrooms, onion and raw potatoes very well, and pour over the meat balls. Cover with aluminum foil and bake at 350°F. for 45 minutes. Then remove the foil and continue to bake for 15 minutes longer. Serve piping hot.

HEARTY CASSEROLE

1 tablespoon butter or margarine
1/2 cup chopped onion
1 pound ground chuck
1/2 pound American process cheese, cut into 1/4" cubes
1 8-ounce package elbow macaroni, cooked in 3 quarts salted, boiling water
1 tablespoon mustard
1 package frozen corn
1/2 teaspoon salt
1/4 teaspoon pepper
1 can condensed tomato soup

Melt the butter in a skillet, add the onion and cook until transparent. Then add the meat and continue to cook until it loses its reddish color. Set aside to cool.

Mix the cheese, macaroni, mustard, corn, salt, pepper and tomato soup. Stir in the mixture of meat and onion. Place in a 1-1/2 quart buttered casserole and bake at 350°F. for 1 hour. Serve piping hot.

WILD RICE AND HAMBURGER CASSEROLE

3/4 cup wild rice
2 cups slightly salted water
1 pound combined beef, veal and pork ground together
1/2 cup chopped onion
1/2 cup celery, chopped fine
1/2 teaspoon salt
1/2 teaspoon Accent
1/2 teaspoon Worcestershire sauce
1 can condensed cream of mushroom soup
1/4 cup sherry wine
1/4 cup grated Parmesan cheese
1 cup quartered canned or fresh mushrooms, if desired

Cook the wild rice in the water until each grain is doubled in size. Drain rice, rinse in warm tap water, and set aside in strainer to drain thoroughly dry.

Sauté the ground meat till brown, add the onion, celery, salt, Accent and Worcestershire sauce. Stir in the wild rice and mushroom soup. Add the wine. Place in a well-greased casserole; sprinkle the cheese over the top. Bake in a 350°F. oven for 1 hour.

Since wild rice and mushrooms complement each other, you may also use a cup of canned or fresh mushrooms in this recipe.

Variations:

Substitute 1/4 cup grated American cheese for the Parmesan cheese.
Substitute 1/4 cup feta (Greek) cheese for the Parmesan cheese.
Substitute 1 can cream of celery soup for the mushroom soup.
Substitute 1 can cream of asparagus soup for the mushroom soup.
Substitute 1 can cream of chicken soup for the mushroom soup.

EGGPLANT, LAMB AND CRACKED WHEAT CASSEROLE

3 tablespoons olive oil
1 pound ground lamb
1/2 cup chopped onion
1/2 cup chopped green pepper
1 #2 can tomatoes
1 medium-sized eggplant, peeled and cut into 1" pieces
2 cloves garlic
1 teaspoon salt
4 twists of pepper mill
1 tablespoon lemon juice
1 teaspoon lemon rind
3/4 cup cracked wheat
1 cup water
1/2 cup Parmesan-Romano cheese

Place 1 tablespoon of the olive oil in a skillet and brown the ground lamb. Add the onion and green pepper and cook until they are glazed and soft. Stir in the tomatoes and set aside.

Meanwhile, in another skillet, heat the remaining 2 tablespoons of olive oil and sauté the eggplant cubes until they are almost tender. Add the garlic, salt, pepper, lemon juice and rind. Cook the cracked wheat in the water until all the kernels are separated, doubled in size and tender. All of the water should be absorbed in the cooking.

Place half of the cracked wheat in the bottom of a well-buttered 2-quart casserole. Put half the lamb mixture over this, then half the eggplant, and repeat the layers with the other half of each. Sprinkle the cheese over the top and place in a 350°F. oven for 30 minutes. Serve piping hot.

You can make variations on this delicious casserole by substituting ground beef, ground ham, or a mixture of ground beef, veal and pork for the lamb.

HAMBURGER AND RICE CASSEROLE

1 pound hamburger
1 teaspoon onion juice or 1 tablespoon onion, chopped very fine
1/2 cup celery, chopped fine
1/4 teaspoon ground black pepper
1 teaspoon salt
Dash of nutmeg
1 8-ounce can tomato sauce
1 egg
2 cups cooked regular rice
1/2 cup dry bread crumbs
1 tablespoon butter or margarine

Put the hamburger into a good-sized mixing bowl; add the onion, celery, black pepper, salt and nutmeg. Mix all very thoroughly; then stir in the tomato sauce.

In another mixing bowl, beat the egg with a rotary beater until light and lemon colored. Add the rice and mix thoroughly. Press half the rice-egg mixture around the sides and over the bottom of a well-greased casserole. Reserve the other half of the rice to go over the top.

Place this casserole under the broiler for 5 minutes, or until the rice begins to brown and is set firmly around the sides. Remove from the oven, and put in the meat mixture carefully, using a rubber spatula to spread it evenly. Cover with the remainder of the rice-egg mixture, and sprinkle the bread crumbs over the top. Dot with the butter or margarine.

Bake at 350°F. for 45 minutes. Just before serving, place under the broiler for a few seconds to brown the crumbs on top.

HAMBURGER CHOW MEIN

1 pound of pork, veal and beef, ground together
6 medium-sized onions in 1/4" slices
2 cups celery, cut in 1/4" slices
1 #2 can of tomatoes
1 #2 can of bean sprouts
1 #2 can of mushroom stems and pieces
1 7-ounce can water chestnuts (optional)
1 tablespoon soy sauce
1 teaspoon bead molasses
1 teaspoon monosodium glutamate
1 #2 can chow mein noodles

Slowly sauté the meat until it is in lumps about the size of hickory nuts, and light brown in color. The pork in the mixture should supply enough fat for sautéing.

Add the onions, celery and tomatoes and simmer slowly for 35 minutes. Do not cover, or celery will lose its green color. Add the bean sprouts, mushrooms, water chestnuts, soy sauce, molasses and monosodium glutamate. Simmer for 10 minutes longer. Heat the noodles in the oven at 250°F. for 10 minutes. Serve the chow mein over the heated noodles.

If you really want to show off, add about 10 sliced almonds and a few cubes of pimento to the recipe and sprinkle a little of each over the top of each serving.

Variations:

Substitute 1 10-1/2-ounce can cream of chicken soup and 1 can of water for the tomatoes.
Substitute 1 10-1/2-ounce can cream of mushroom soup and 1 can of water for the tomatoes.
Substitute 1 10-1/2-ounce can cream of celery soup and 1 can of water for the tomatoes.
Substitute 1 8-ounce package medium-sized egg noodles, boiled until tender, for the chow mein noodles.
Substitute 3 cups cooked rice for the chow mein noodles.
Substitute 2 packages frozen French-fried onion rings for the chow mein noodles.

ONIONS AND HAMBURGER, MILAN STYLE

4 large Bermuda onions, or 8 medium-sized onions
1 pound hamburger
8 soda crackers, soaked in enough milk to soften
1/4 cup Parmesan cheese
2 3" diameter ginger snaps, broken into small pieces
1/4 teaspoon salt
1/4 teaspoon pepper, or 4 twists pepper mill
1/2 teaspoon monosodium glutamate
2 tablespoons chopped parsley
2 eggs, beaten until lemon yellow
1/2 teaspoon paprika

Very carefully peel the onions, removing only the first layer of the peeling. Cut a 1/2" slice from the top of the onion—enough so that all the inner rings are exposed. Stick a toothpick into the side of the onion straight through the center. If the onions are very large, insert toothpicks from each side. This is to keep the onions from losing their shape during cooking. Place the onions in a saucepan, cover with water and boil very slowly for 20 minutes. Set them aside in their own liquid to cool so that you can handle them with ease.

Brown the hamburger in a skillet until it is all separated and in small pieces. Now remove the toothpicks from the onions and using a teaspoon, carefully scoop out the centers. Leave about 1/2" wall. Add to the hamburger the onion centers you scooped out.

Cook the hamburger and onion centers until the onion breaks apart and is glazed. Remove from the heat and stir in the drained soda crackers. Stir in the Parmesan cheese. Next add the pieces of ginger snaps and stir until they are completely dissolved. Add the salt, pepper, monosodium glutamate and parsley. When the mixture has cooled, add half of the beaten eggs. Reserve the other half until later.

Using a teaspoon, pack the filling into each onion shell, taking care not to break through the outer walls. Place the onions in a buttered baking dish. Pour the remainder of the beaten eggs, by tablespoonfuls, over the onions. Sprinkle a little of the paprika over them. Place in a preheated 350°F. oven and bake for 35 minutes.

GLAZED BURGERS

1 pound hamburger
1 tablespoon minced onion
1 tablespoon minced parsley
1 can dehydrated mushroom soup
1 egg, beaten until lemon yellow
2 tablespoons butter or margarine

Glaze

1 cup apple butter
1 tablespoon grated orange rind

Mix the hamburger with the onion, parsley, mushroom soup and egg. Form into 8 patties. Melt the butter or margarine in a skillet and brown the patties well on each side.

To make the glaze, put the apple butter and orange rind in the skillet. Simmer for 15 minutes, turning each patty several times so it will be well covered with the glaze.

Serve on hot hamburger buns.

BURGERS IN FOIL

1 pound hamburger
1/2 teaspoon salt
4 twists of pepper mill
1 tablespoon Worcestershire sauce
1 tablespoon catsup
1/4 pound butter or margarine
1/8 teaspoon thyme
10-15 dill seeds
1 teaspoon soy sauce
8 hamburger buns

Mix the hamburger, salt, pepper, Worcestershire sauce and catsup very well. Form into 8 patties. Broil on each side enough to brown. Melt the butter or margarine, add the thyme, dill seeds and soy sauce. Brush the bottoms and tops of the hamburger buns generously with the flavored butter. Place a meat patty in each bun. Wrap tightly in squares of aluminum foil. Place in a 350°F. oven for 30 minutes. If onions on hamburgers are a favorite, put a large onion slice on each burger before placing in the bun.

These burgers are equally good served on an outdoor grill. All ingredients can be prepared ahead of time, and then heated around the edge of the grill while corn or potatoes are roasting.

UPSIDE-DOWN SANDWICHES

1/2 cup bread crumbs
1 tablespoon dehydrated onion
1/2 cup milk
1 pound ground beef
1 egg, beaten to a lemon yellow
2 tablespoons capers, chopped very fine
4 tablespoons butter or margarine
6 slices white bread

Place the bread crumbs and onion in the milk and let the crumbs swell and absorb all of the milk. Place the meat in a bowl and mix with the bread crumbs and milk. Add the egg and the chopped capers. Mix all very well.

Melt the butter in a skillet and place each slice of bread in it until it is golden brown on one side. Spread a generous portion of the meat mixture on the unbrowned side of the bread. Place the bread, meat side down, in the skillet and cook until the meat is browned. Serve piping hot.

BLEU CHEESE BURGERS

1 pound ground chuck
1 medium onion, chopped very fine
1 tablespoon Worcestershire sauce
1 teaspoon sugar
1/2 teaspoon Accent
1 teaspoon prepared mustard
1/4 cup tomato sauce or 1/4 cup chili sauce
6 hamburger buns
6 tablespoons soft butter or margarine
1/2 cup Bleu cheese mixed in 1/2 cup mayonnaise

Mix the ground meat, onion, Worcestershire sauce, sugar, Accent, mustard and tomato sauce very thoroughly. Set aside to allow the flavors to blend. This meat mixture can be made several hours before serving, or even the day before.

Butter the hamburger bun halves and place under the broiler until they are toasted a golden brown.

Place 1 heaping tablespoonful of the cheese and mayonnaise mixture in the center of each bun half. Form the meat into 1/2″ thick patties the size of the buns; place the meat patty over the Bleu cheese mixture. Press the edges of each patty so that the cheese mixture is completely sealed inside. Put under the broiler for 15 minutes, or until the meat is completely browned. Serve piping hot.

This will yield 12 half buns, or 2 portions per person.

TEENAGERS' SPECIAL SANDWICHES

1 tablespoon dehydrated onion
2 tablespoons water
1/4 teaspoon nutmeg
1/2 teaspoon salt
1/4 teaspoon pepper
1/4 teaspoon cardamon
1 pound ground round steak or very lean ground chuck
10 slices white bread
4 tablespoons butter or margarine
2 eggs
1/4 cup milk

Place the dehydrated onion in the water for 10 minutes. Then mix it very thoroughly with the nutmeg, salt, pepper, cardamon and meat. Spread the meat mixture on one side of each of 5 slices of bread. Press the remaining 5 slices of bread tightly over the meat mixture.

Melt the butter or margarine in a large skillet. Meanwhile, beat the egg in the milk. Dip the sandwiches in the beaten egg mixture and then put the sandwiches in the skillet and fry slowly until each side is browned. Serve with pickle slices.

TEENS' RIB LINERS

1 pound hamburger
1 tablespoon butter or margarine
1 teaspoon salt
1/2 teaspoon pepper
1/4 cup chopped onion
2 cloves of garlic, minced
1 #2 can red kidney beans, drained and chopped very fine
1/2 teaspoon oregano
1/2 teaspoon chili powder
8 hamburger buns

Brown the hamburger in the butter or margarine, add the salt, pepper, onion and garlic. Stir in the kidney beans. Add the oregano and the chili powder and simmer for 10 minutes longer. Put a generous spoonful of this mixture on each bun and serve with potato chips and pickles.

This is an ideal teen-age treat because it can be kept warm in the top of a double boiler and served whenever needed. This is also a good item to freeze. You can double or even triple the recipe and freeze the extra portions against that day when you are suddenly invaded by a tribe of hungry youngsters.

SLOPPY JOE

There are many versions of "Sloppy Joe" sandwiches, but the following three recipes are our favorites. Once you get the knack of making this teen-agers' delight, you will think of many variations. Sloppy Joes take only a short time to prepare, and being a mother who knows what to serve while the Beatles are bleating will mark you as "cool" forever.

2 pounds hamburger
1 large onion, diced
1/2 cup catsup
1 cup water
1 7-ounce can mushroom stems and pieces, drained
1/2 teaspoon salt
1/4 teaspoon pepper
1 10-1/2-ounce can minestrone soup
8 hamburger buns

Brown the hamburger and break it apart until it is quite fine. Add the onion and continue to cook until the onion is transparent and glazed. Add the catsup, water, mushrooms, salt, pepper and soup. Cook over low heat for 25 minutes. Stir from time to time to prevent scorching.

Place heaping spoonfuls in the middle of each hamburger bun and serve.

SLOPPIER JOES

2 pounds hamburger
1 large onion, diced
1 #2 can tomatoes
8 hamburger buns
6 slices bacon, diced and fried crisp
1/2 cup grated American cheese

Brown the hamburger until it is all broken apart; add the diced onion and cook until it is glazed. Add the tomatoes and simmer for 25 minutes without a cover. Stir from time to time to prevent scorching.

Remove from heat and place a heaping spoonful of the meat mixture on the bottom of each hamburger bun. (Set aside the tops temporarily.) Sprinkle with the crisp bacon, then top with the grated cheese. Place under the broiler until the cheese is melted. Cover with bun tops, and serve.

BEEF WELLINGTON

1 4-lb fillet of beef
Salt to taste
Pepper to taste
4 T butter, softened
1 can (4 oz) chopped mushrooms, drained
2 cans (4 oz each) liver pâté
1/4 tsp rosemary
1 recipe rich or puff paste
1 egg
1 tsp milk

Season beef with salt and pepper. Spread with butter, place in a roasting pan, and roast in a 500° F. oven 25 to 30 minutes for rare. Remove from oven and cool. Meanwhile, combine mushrooms, liver pâté, and rosemary. When beef is cool spread with pâté mixture. Roll out pastry about 1/4 inch thick into a rectangle large enough to wrap beef and have a few inches in reserve. Wrap beef in pastry, trim edges of pastry, moisten with water and seal. Place on aluminum foil lined cookie sheet, seam side down. Brush crust with egg beaten with milk. Roll out trimmed pastry and cut into narrow strips. Lay across dough-wrapped beef in a lattice pattern and brush again with egg mixture. Prick crust. Bake in 450° F. oven for 15 minutes, or until pastry is delicately browned.

Serves 8 to 10.

BEEF CARBONNADE

1/4 C cooking oil
2 lbs lean beef, cut into 1-inch cubes
Salt to taste
Pepper to taste
2 lbs onions, sliced
2 garlic cloves, minced
2/3 C beef stock
1 bottle (12 oz) beer
1 T brown sugar
1 tsp parsley
1 tsp thyme
1 T arrowroot
2 T cold water

Heat oil in a heavy skillet. Brown meat on all sides. Add salt and pepper to taste. Remove meat from skillet to casserole. Brown onions and garlic in skillet, and add to casserole. In saucepan combine stock, beer, brown sugar, parsley, and thyme. Pour over mixture in casserole. Cover tightly and bake in 325° F. oven for 2-1/2 hours. Mix arrowroot with cold water. Stir into casserole and correct seasoning. Heat 15 minutes longer, or until gravy thickens.

Serves 8.

CASSEROLES

EGGS ITALIAN

1 cup purple Italian onion, sliced 1/8 inch thick
1/2 cup soft butter
2 cups milk
8 hard-cooked eggs, sliced 1/4 inch thick
2 tablespoons parsley, finely chopped
1/4 cup grated Parmesan cheese
1 tablespoon lemon juice
1/2 teaspoon salt
1/4 teaspoon freshly ground pepper
4 (additional) raw eggs, beaten until lemon yellow
3 medium-sized tomatoes, washed and sliced 1/2 inch thick (8 slices needed)
1/2 cup all-purpose flour
2 tablespoons olive oil
4 slices, toasted, enriched white bread, lightly buttered, or 2 English muffins, halved, toasted and buttered

Melt the butter in the top of a double boiler. Add the sliced onions and sauté over low heat until they are limp and transparent and just slightly browned. Add the milk and continue to cook over low heat until just below the scalding point. Remove from heat and stir in the sliced eggs, parsley, grated cheese, lemon juice, salt and pepper. Mix well.

Add 1/2 cup of the hot milk mixture to the beaten eggs and mix well; then add the beaten egg mixture to the hard-cooked egg mixture.

Place over slowly boiling water and cook, stirring constantly, until the mixture has thickened. Turn off the heat, cover and set aside while you prepare the tomatoes.

Dip the tomato slices in the flour. Place the olive oil in a skillet over moderate heat and sauté the tomato slices until they are a golden brown. Do not overcook, as they should retain their round shape. Place two browned, hot tomato slices on a slice of toast; then top with the hot, hard-cooked egg mixture. Serve at once. Serves 4.

EGG PANCAKE SUPPER

6 hard-cooked eggs, peeled
6 strips bacon, diced in 1/4-inch cubes
1/4 cup chopped green onion
1/4 cup parsley, finely chopped
1 cup prepared pancake mix
1-1/2 cups milk
1/3 cup melted butter
1 (additional) well-beaten egg
1/2 cup sour cream
1/4 cup grated Parmesan cheese

Chop the hard-cooked eggs until they are the consistency of hamburger.

Place the bacon cubes in a skillet and sauté until they are crisp and golden brown. Remove the bacon cubes with a slotted spoon and drain on absorbent paper. Add the green onion to the remaining bacon fat and cook until slightly browned. Remove the onion with a slotted spoon and add to the chopped eggs along with the parsley and drained bacon cubes. Mix well. Mix the milk and the pancake flour; beat until free of lumps. Add the beaten egg and 1 tablespoon of the melted butter and mix again. Stir one half of the chopped egg mixture into the pancake batter. Set aside for 5 minutes for the flavors to unite.

Using the reserved bacon fat, fry large-sized pancakes, about 4 inches in diameter, on a hot griddle. As soon as the pancakes are golden brown on both sides, sprinkle with a portion of the remaining chopped egg mixture. Roll up the pancake jelly-roll fashion and place in a buttered, oblong, casserole dish. Place the rolled-up pancakes closely together; keep warm in a 250°F. oven until you have completed all the pancakes.

Brush the tops of the pancake rolls with the remaining butter and then srpead the sour cream over the top. Sprinkle the surface with the grated Parmesan cheese. Return the dish to a 350°F. oven and bake for 10 minutes or until the cheese has melted and becomes slightly golden. Serve at once, piping hot. Serves 6.

EAT-MORE CASSEROLE

1 pound hamburger
1/2 pound elbow macaroni
1 cup chopped onion or 1/2 cup dehydrated onion soaked in 1/2 cup water
1 #2 can tomatoes
1 cup tomato sauce
1/4 teaspoon salt
1/4 teaspoon pepper
1/4 teaspoon garlic powder
1 teaspoon Accent
1 can niblet-style corn with pimento, drained

Sauté the hamburger until a golden brown. Meanwhile, boil the macaroni in slightly salted water until tender. Drain the macaroni and combine it with the hamburger; add the onion, tomatoes, tomato sauce, salt, pepper, garlic powder and Accent to the meat. Last, fold in the corn.

Place this mixture in a 1-1/2-quart buttered casserole and put into a preheated 350°F. oven; bake for 45 minutes.

WALNUT-MEAT BALL CASSEROLE

2 pounds hamburger
1 cup chopped walnuts
1 cup bread crumbs
3 eggs, beaten to a lemon yellow
3/4 cup milk
1 package dehydrated French onion soup
1/2 cup boiling water

Mix the hamburger, walnuts, bread crumbs, eggs and milk thoroughly. Form into 1" diameter meat balls and brown them a few at a time. Shaking the skillet back and forth slowly over the flame will assure even browning.

Mix the dehydrated onion soup with the boiling water and pour over the meat balls. Place in a preheated 350°F. oven for a half hour. Add more water if necessary. Should you desire additional gravy, remove meat balls, add 3/4 cup of water with tablespoon cornstarch mixed in it. Simmer for 5 minutes longer, and return meat balls to the gravy.

MADRID RICE CASSEROLE

3 slices bacon, cut into 1/4" pieces
1/2 cup onion, chopped fine
1-1/2 pounds hamburger
1/4 teaspoon thyme
1/4 teaspoon sweet basil
1 #2 can tomato juice
1-1/2 cups precooked rice
1 green pepper, cut into 1/4" pieces
1/2 teaspoon paprika

Sauté the bacon in a skillet until slightly browned. Pour away most of the fat; add the onion and continue to sauté until the onion is slightly transparent. Add the hamburger to the onion and bacon, along with the thyme and basil. Cook for a few minutes longer, until the meat loses its reddish color. Remove from heat, and add the tomato juice. Stir in the rice just as it comes from the package. Add most of the green pepper, reserving a few pieces for later. Place the entire mixture in a 1-1/2-quart casserole and sprinkle the paprika over the top.

Place the casserole in a 350° F. oven and bake for 35 minutes, uncovered. Five minutes before removing from the oven, sprinkle the remaining green pepper over the top for color. Serve right from the casserole used to bake in.

I usually bake a double quantity of this casserole, one for serving and one for freezing. This is a satisfying main dish for a hurry-up meal.

Variations:

Add 1 package frozen okra.
Add 1 package frozen zucchini squash.
Add 1 package frozen French-style green beans.
Omit the green pepper and use 1 8-ounce can of mushrooms.
Add 1 package frozen niblet-style corn.

CHICKEN AND WILD RICE CASSEROLE

1 pkg (6 oz) long grain wild rice
1/4 C butter
1/3 C onion, chopped
1/3 C flour
1 tsp salt
1/4 tsp pepper
1 C half-and-half cream
1 C chicken broth
2 C cooked cubed chicken
1/4 C fresh parsley, minced
1/4 C almonds, chopped

Cook rice according to directions on package. Melt butter in frying pan. Sauté onions until golden. Add flour, salt and pepper to onions. Mix well. Gradually add cream and chicken broth, stirring constantly. Cook until thickened. To cooked rice add the sauce, chicken, parsley and almonds. Mix well and pour into a greased casserole. Bake in a 425° F. oven for 30 minutes.

Serves 8.

SESAME DRUMSTICKS

6 T butter
1 egg
1/2 C milk
1/2 C flour
1 tsp salt
1/4 tsp pepper
1/4 C sesame seeds
1/4 tsp ginger
12 chicken drumsticks

Preheat oven to 375°F. Melt butter in large shallow baking dish. In a small bowl, beat egg slightly and add milk. In separate bowl combine flour, salt, pepper, sesame seeds and ginger. Dip drumsticks in egg mixture, then in sesame mixture. Roll in melted butter in baking dish. Bake in 375°F. oven for 1-1/2 hours or until crisp and tender.

Serves 6.

CHICKEN TETRAZZINI

1 pkg (8 oz) thin spaghetti
1 can (10-1/2 oz) condensed cream of chicken soup
1/2 C milk
2 C diced cooked chicken
1 can (4 oz) sliced mushrooms
1/4 C grated Parmesan cheese

Cook spaghetti as directed on package. Drain and place in a buttered 2-quart casserole. Mix soup and milk. Add diced chicken and drained mushrooms. Combine chicken mixture with spaghetti. Sprinkle cheese on top. Bake in a 350°F. oven for 30 minutes.

Serves 6 to 8.

TURKEY ROLL WITH STUFFING CASSEROLE

1 boned turkey roll (5 to 7 lbs)
1/4 C Chinese-style sparerib or duck sauce

Place turkey roll in small roasting pan and roast according to package directions. One hour before turkey is finished baste with Chinese-style sauce. Serve with stuffing casserole (below).

Serves 8 to 10.

STUFFING CASSEROLE

1 stick margarine
1/2 C onion, minced
1/2 C celery stalks and leaves, chopped
4 C plain white bread cubes
1 egg
Milk (to make 1/2 cup with egg)
2 T salt
1/2 tsp pepper
1 tsp poultry seasoning (or more to taste if desired)

Melt margarine in large frying pan. Sauté onions and celery until golden. Add half of the bread cubes to frying pan and heat. Beat egg slightly in measuring cup. Add milk to measure one half cup. Mix well. Place remaining half of bread cubes in large mixing bowl. Sprinkle seasonings on dry bread cubes. Add egg mixture and contents of frying pan. Toss lightly. Put in large greased casserole, cover and bake in oven with turkey for the last hour.

Serves 8 to 10.

VEAL SCALLOPS IN CREAM SAUCE

1/3 C flour
1 tsp salt
1/2 tsp pepper
1 tsp paprika
2 lbs veal, cut into scallops
1/4 C butter
3/4 C white wine
1 C light cream

Combine flour, salt, pepper, and paprika. Dredge veal scallops in flour mixture. Melt butter in frying pan and brown veal lightly. Pour in wine and simmer until wine has almost evaporated. Pour in cream and simmer gently, covered, for 20 minutes longer. Transfer meat to serving dish. Pour sauce over meat and serve.

Serves 6 to 8.

CRAB DELIGHT

1 pkg (10 oz) frozen chopped spinach
1 can (10-1/2 oz) condensed cream of mushroom soup
1/4 C flour
1/2 C milk
1/2 tsp nutmeg
1 can (4 oz) mushroom pieces, drained
1 C Swiss cheese, shredded
2 cans (7-1/2 oz) crabmeat, drained and flaked, any shell and
    cartilage discarded
1/4 C almonds, diced
1/4 C white wine
4 T butter
1-1/2 C bread cubes

Cook spinach as directed on package, and then drain well. Spread spinach in bottom of a 2-quart casserole. In a saucepan, combine soup, flour, milk, and nutmeg. Add the mushrooms. Cook over medium heat until thickened, stirring constantly. Add the Swiss cheese and stir until melted. Add the crabmeat, almonds and the white wine. Pour this mixture over the spinach in the casserole. Melt the butter in a small pan. Combine the butter with the bread cubes and sprinkle on top of the casserole mixture. Bake at 400° F. for 25 minutes, or until the bread cubes are a toasted golden brown.

Serves 6 to 8.

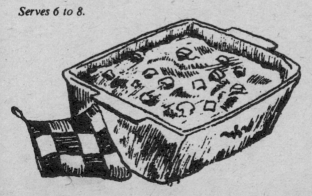

CRABMEAT BISCUIT BAKE

1/2 C green pepper, chopped
1/2 C onion, chopped
1/4 C butter
1/4 C flour
1 tsp dry mustard
1 can (1 lb) tomatoes
1 T Worcestershire sauce
2 pkgs (6 oz) frozen crabmeat, thawed and drained, any shell
   and cartilage discarded
1 C American cheese, shredded
1/4 C sherry
1 can packaged refrigerator biscuits

Sauté green pepper and onion in butter in a saucepan until
tender. Blend in the flour and the dry mustard. Gradually stir in
the tomatoes and Worcestershire sauce. Cook over medium
heat until mixture boils and thickens. Add crabmeat, and
simmer covered for 10 minutes. Stir in the cheese and sherry.
Pour into a 2-quart casserole. Open the can of biscuits, separate
each biscuit and cut into quarters. Arrange on top of the
casserole mixture with the points facing up. Bake at 375° F. for
20 to 25 minutes or until biscuits are done.

Serves 8.

CRAB LOUIS

1 head iceberg lettuce
3 C crabmeat, cooked and cleaned
1 ripe avocado, peeled and cut into slices
1 jar (6 oz) marinated artichoke hearts
3 tomatoes, cut into eighths
1 lemon, cut into 6 wedges
6 eggs, hard cooked and cut in half

Tear lettuce into bite-sized pieces and make a bed on 6 individual places. Arrange crabmeat, cartilage removed, in center of each plate. Divide avocado slices and artichoke hearts evenly between each plate. Garnish each portion with tomato wedges, 1 lemon wedge, and 2 egg halves. Just before serving make *Louis Salad Dressing* (below).

LOUIS SALAD DRESSING

1/2 C heavy cream
1 C mayonnaise

Whip heavy cream until stiff and then fold in the mayonnaise. Pour salad dressing over each individual salad and serve immediately.

Serves 6.

SALMON SALAD MOLD

1 T (1 envelope) unflavored gelatin
2 T cold water
1/2 T flour
1-1/2 T sugar
1 tsp salt
1 tsp dry mustard
1/4 tsp pepper
2 eggs
3/4 C milk
1/4 C vinegar
1-1/2 T melted butter
1-1/2 C flaked salmon
1/2 C heavy cream, whipped
8 large pitted black olives, halved

Soften gelatin in the cold water. Mix the flour, sugar, salt, dry mustard and pepper in the top of a double boiler. Add the eggs and stir until well blended. Gradually add milk and vinegar. Cook over hot water until the mixture thickens, stirring constantly. Add butter and the softened gelatin and stir until the gelatin is dissolved. Remove from heat. Stir in the salmon. Chill, stirring occasionally. When mixture starts to thicken, fold in the whipped cream and pour into a mold. Chill until firm. Unmold on a bed of lettuce and garnish with the black olives.

Serves 8 to 10.

SHRIMP AND RICE a la SUISSE

1 C long grain rice
3 T butter, melted
1 medium onion, chopped
1 green pepper, chopped
1 clove garlic, minced
1-1/2 tsp salt
2-1/2 C hot water
2 lbs raw shrimp, peeled and deveined
1/2 lb Swiss cheese, shredded
1/3 C evaporated milk

Brown rice in the melted butter. Add onion, pepper and garlic and cook until onion is golden. Add salt and hot water, place shrimp on top and cover. Cook over low heat 30 to 40 minutes or until the rice is done. Check that water does not cook away. Combine the Swiss cheese and the evaporated milk in a saucepan and cook, stirring constantly, over low heat until the cheese melts and the mixture is hot. Serve the cheese mixture in a separate sauce dish.

Serves 6 to 8.

CURRIED SHRIMP

2-1/2 lbs raw shrimp in shells, or 1-1/2 lbs cleaned
1/2 tsp salt
1/4 tsp pepper
1 onion, sliced
1 lemon, sliced
1/4 C butter
1-1/2 T curry powder
3/4 C onions, chopped
3/4 C apples, peeled and diced
1 beef bouillon cube
1 C hot water
1/2 T cornstarch
3 T cold water
1/2 C light cream

Place shrimp in a large pan with water to cover. Add the salt, pepper, onion slices, and lemon slices. Bring to a boil and cook until the shrimp are pink, about 1 to 2 minutes. Drain and set aside. When cool, remove shrimp shells and devein. Melt butter in a large skillet. Add the curry, chopped onions, and the apples. Sauté this mixture for 10 minutes, stirring constantly. Add the bouillon cube dissolved in the hot water. Simmer, stirring constantly, for 10 minutes. Combine cornstarch with the cold water and add to the mixture in the skillet. Stir until mixture thickens. Add the shrimp and the cream to the skillet mixture. Mix together until thickened, but do not overcook.

Serves 8.

EGG FOO YOUNG WITH SHRIMP

1/2 cup onion, coarsely chopped
1 clove garlic, finely minced
1 tablespoon peanut oil
1 cup cooked, deveined shrimp cut into 3/4-inch pieces
6 eggs, beaten until slightly bubbly
1/2 teaspoon Accent
1/2 teaspoon salt
1/8 teaspoon freshly ground pepper
2 tablespoons (additional) peanut oil

Sauce:
1/4 cup butter
1/4 cup flour
1 teaspoon granulated sugar
2 chicken bouillon cubes dissolved in 1 cup boiling water
1/4 cup soy sauce
1 cup canned bean sprouts, drained

Place the onion, garlic and oil in a skillet over moderate heat and sauté until the onion becomes limp and transparent. Add the pieces of shrimp and sauté them until they begin to turn a golden brown. Remove from the heat and allow to cool.

Mix the eggs, Accent, salt and pepper thoroughly. Add the shrimp and onion mixture and mix all well.

Place the additional peanut oil in a skillet which has a tightly fitting cover over low heat; add the egg mixture and cook very slowly, covered, until the eggs are firm. Fold in half and place on an oven-proof platter under the broiler until a golden brown.

For the sauce, melt the butter in the same skillet. Stir in the flour until smoothly blended. Add the sugar, hot bouillon water and soy sauce. Cook over very low heat, stirring constantly, until the mixture has thickened. Add the bean sprouts and continue to cook a few seconds longer until heated through. Pour the sauce over the shrimp omelet and serve. Serves 6.

EGG CROQUETTES

8 hard-cooked eggs, chilled and peeled
1 4-ounce can mushroom stems and pieces, drained
1/2 teaspoon salt
1/4 teaspoon pepper
3 tablespoons butter
3 tablespoons all-purpose flour
1-1/2 cups milk
1 (additional) raw egg
1/4 cup (additional) milk
1-1/2 cups fine bread or cracker crumbs
Vegetable oil for deep frying
1 tablespoon parsley, finely chopped

Chop the eggs and mushrooms until they are the consistency of coarse corn meal. Add the salt and pepper and mix well.

Melt the butter in a saucepan over low heat; stir in the flour. When the mixture is smooth and free of lumps, add the milk and continue to cook over very low heat, stirring constantly, until the mixture is thick and creamy.

Add 1/2 cup of the thick cream sauce to the chopped eggs and mushrooms. Reserve the rest of the cream sauce until later. Mix the eggs, mushrooms and cream sauce together well and spread over the bottom of a flat pan. Place in the coldest part of the refrigerator for 1 hour to become firm and solid.

When chilled and firm, form the mixture into balls about the size of an egg. Beat the additional raw egg until frothy, add the additional milk; mix well. Dip each ball into the egg-milk mixture and then roll in the bread or cracker crumbs until completely covered.

Place the croquettes in the hot oil (375° F.) and fry until they are a golden brown. Remove from the oil and place on a paper towel to drain.

Reheat the remainder of the cream sauce over slowly boiling water in a double boiler. Serve the croquettes with a portion of the hot cream sauce. Sprinkle with the minced parsley for added flavor and color. Serves 4.

EGG, MUSHROOM, SPINACH MOLD

4 eggs, separated
2 10-ounce packages frozen, chopped spinach, thawed to room
    temperature
1/4 cup butter
1/4 cup all-purpose flour
1/2 cup half-and-half cream
1/2 teaspoon salt
1/4 teaspoon pepper
1/4 teaspoon grated nutmeg
1 10-ounce can mushroom stems and pieces
1 10-ounce can cream of mushroom soup
4 (additional) hard-cooked eggs

Beat the egg yolks until they are lemon colored. Set aside.
Beat the egg whites until they stand in peaks. Set aside.

Melt the butter in a large skillet and add the flour; mix well
and continue to cook until the mixture bubbles. Stir in the
cream, salt, pepper and nutmeg. Continue to cook, stirring
constantly, until the mixture is thick. Take two tablespoons of
the mixture and add to the egg yolks. Mix well and then add the
egg yolks to the cream mixture. Mix thoroughly and cook for a
few seconds. Add the chopped spinach and mix until all is
smoothly blended. Remove from the heat and allow to cool.

Fold the beaten egg whites into the spinach mixture, taking
care to retain all of the air. Spoon the mixture into a 10-inch
generously buttered ring mold. Place the mold, uncovered, in a
pan of hot water in a 350°F. oven and bake for 35 minutes or
until the mold is firmly set and slightly puffed up.

Meanwhile, heat the mushroom soup, just as it comes from
the can, and the mushroom stems and pieces over rapidly
boiling water in a double boiler. Five minutes before serving,
add the sliced hard-cooked eggs to the mushroom soup and
allow them to heat through.

Loosen the spinach ring with a sharp knife and unmold on to
a heated platter. Pour the egg-mushroom soup mixture into the
center. Serve piping hot. Serves 6.

VIENNESE POACHED EGGS

8 eggs
1 cup half-and-half cream
4 tablespoons butter
16 slices thin, lean bacon
8 slices enriched white bread
Salt and pepper to taste

For true Viennese-style Eggs, you should use a large European-style egg poacher. If you do not own one, these eggs can be made in individual custard cups.

Butter 4 poachers or custard cups lavishly. Place 1/4 cup of the cream in each of the egg poacher cups over rapidly boiling water. When the cream has reached the scalding hot stage, break the eggs into a saucer, one by one, and slip two into each cup of hot cream. Cover and poach until the eggs are firm and slightly glazed over.

Broil the bacon until it is crisp and golden. Toast the slices of bread. Butter four of the slices and place in the oven to keep warm. Place the remaining unbuttered toast on heated serving plates; top each piece of toast with four of the slices of crisp bacon. Top the bacon with two of the poached eggs and their hot cream. Season each serving to taste. Serve at once with buttered hot slices of toast. Serves 4, allowing 2 eggs per person.

EGG AND CLAM BAKE

6 eggs
4 cups coarse cracker crumbs
1/4 cup onion, finely chopped
2 cups milk
2 7-1/2-ounce cans minced clams, with their juice
1/4 cup melted butter

Beat the eggs until they are thoroughly mixed and bubbly. Add the cracker crumbs, chopped onion and milk and mix again. Add the minced clams and their juice and stir until the clams are evenly distributed throughout the mixture.

Pour into a buttered baking dish, smooth down the surface and drizzle the melted butter over the top.

Bake in a 350°F. oven for 40 minutes or until the top is a delicate golden brown. Serve piping hot. Serves 6.

SALMON LOAF WITH EGGS

1 1-pound can salmon
3 eggs
1/2 cup milk
1/4 teaspoon salt
1/8 teaspoon pepper
1 tablespoon onion, finely minced
1 teaspoon lemon juice
3 cups Special K cereal

Sauce:
1/4 cup butter
1/4 cup all-purpose flour
1 cup milk
1/4 cup salmon liquid
3 (additional) hard-cooked eggs, peeled and finely chopped
1 tablespoon lemon juice
1/4 cup parsley, finely chopped

Drain the salmon and reserve the juice. Remove any skin and bones and then flake the salmon quite finely with a fork.

Beat the raw eggs until they are light and lemon colored. Add the eggs to the flaked salmon along with the milk, salt, pepper, onion and lemon juice. Mix all thoroughly. Add the cereal and mix again. Place the mixture in a lavishly-buttered loaf pan; bake in a 325° F. oven for 1 hour.

Melt the butter in a saucepan; stir in the flour and cook over low heat until the mixture begins to bubble. Add the milk and the salmon liquid. Continue to cook over low heat, stirring constantly, until the mixture has thickened.

Remove the sauce from the heat and stir in the chopped eggs and lemon juice.

Loosen the salmon loaf with a sharp knife and invert on to a heated platter. Pour the egg sauce over the loaf. Garnish the top with the finely-chopped parsley. Cut into generous slices and serve each slice with a portion of the sauce. Serves 6.

DOUBLE DEVILED EGGS

8 hard-cooked eggs, chilled and peeled
1/4 cup mayonnaise
1 teaspoon onion juice
1 teaspoon yellow prepared mustard
1/2 teaspoon A-1 Sauce
1 2-1/4-ounce can deviled ham
1/8 teaspoon freshly ground pepper
16 sprigs parsley

Cut the eggs in half lengthwise. Place the yolks in a bowl and set the whites aside.

Mash the egg yolks with a fork until they are the consistency of coarse corn meal. Add the mayonnaise, onion juice, mustard and A-1 sauce. Mix all well and then add the deviled ham and pepper and mix again.

Mount up a portion of the mixture in each of the waiting egg white halves. Refrigerate at least 30 minutes. Place a sprig of parsley in the center of each egg and serve. Serves 8, allowing two egg halves per each serving.

MIMOSA EGGS

6 hard-cooked eggs, peeled
1 cup mayonnaise
2 tablespoons minced parsley
6 slices enriched white bread, toasted

Preheat the oven to 350°F.

Spread 1/4 cup of the mayonnaise over the bottom of a pie pan with a rubber spoon. Sprinkle 1 tablespoon of the minced parsley over the mayonnaise.

Cut the eggs in half lengthwise. Place the halves, yolk side down, in the pie pan. Spread the remainder of the mayonnaise over the tops of the eggs and sprinkle with the remaining tablespoon of parsley.

Place the eggs in the preheated 350°F. oven for 5 minutes or until the mayonnaise just begins to bubble. Serve at once by placing two egg halves on a slice of toast, top with a portion of the hot mayonnaise. Serves 6.

EGG AND SOUR CREAM SCRAMBLE

6 eggs
1/2 cup thick dairy sour cream
1/2 teaspoon salt
1/8 teaspoon freshly ground pepper
1/4 teaspoon prepared yellow mustard
3 tablespoons butter

Beat the eggs until just broken up and mixed. Add the sour cream, salt, pepper and mustard and beat again until thoroughly mixed.

Melt the butter in a skillet over moderate heat until it just begins to sizzle. Add the egg mixture, lower the heat and cook until the edge begins to thicken. Stir from the edges and the bottom as the eggs become firm. When the eggs are firm, but not dry, transfer to a heated platter and serve. Serves 4.

FRIED EGGS, ITALIAN STYLE

6 eggs
1/4 cup virgin olive oil
Salt and pepper to taste

If you have never had an egg sautéed in good olive oil, your taste buds are missing a real thrill. The selection of the olive oil for frying the eggs is most important. The olive oil should be from the first pressing; the flavor of this type oil is usually sweeter and more delicious than some of the cheaper grades which come from subsequent pressings.

Heat the olive oil over low heat in a skillet which has a tightly fitting cover. When the oil separates and runs to the edges of the pan, break each egg into a saucer and slip it carefully into the hot oil. Sprinkle all the eggs with salt and pepper to taste.

Cover tightly and cook over very low heat for 4 minutes or until the eggs are set; the white should be firm and the yolk shiny and slightly coated. Carefully transfer the eggs to a large heated platter or to individual plates and serve at once.

Buttered toast is excellent with this dish; however, if you want to be completely Italian, fry some slices of white bread in the remaining olive oil until they are a delicate golden brown. Serves 6, allowing 1 egg per person.

BREAKFAST BEEF AND EGG SCRAMBLE

1 6-ounce jar dried beef
1 cup boiling water
2 tablespoons butter
6 eggs
1/8 teaspoon freshly ground pepper
1/4 cup milk

Snip the dried beef into 1/8-inch strips with a kitchen shears. Pour the boiling water over the beef and let stand for 1 minute. Drain through a fine sieve. Press against the bottom and sides of the sieve to remove all the water.

Melt the butter in a skillet over moderate heat until it is sizzling. Add the dried beef and sauté over moderate heat until the beef is slightly crisp.

Beat the eggs at low speed or with a fork until the whites and yolks are evenly mixed. Add the pepper and milk and continue to beat until mixed thoroughly. Pour the eggs over the sautéed dried beef. Turn the heat back to very low. Cook, stirring occasionally, until the eggs are firm, but not dry. Place on a heated platter and serve at once. Serves 4.

EGGS IN A CLOAK

6 eggs, separated
1/4 cup butter
1 tablespoon parsley, finely chopped
1/2 teaspoon salt
1/8 teaspoon pepper

Using half of the butter, grease a 10-inch round baking dish. Slip the yolks into the buttered baking dish; tilt the dish from side to side so that they spread evenly over the bottom. Dot the yolks with the remainder of the butter.

Beat the egg whites until they just begin to stand in peaks. Add the parsley, salt and pepper and beat for 1 second longer.

Using a rubber spoon, gently spread the egg white mixture over the yolks. Place in a 350°F. oven for 5 minutes or until the whites are delicate golden brown. Serve at once, piping hot. Serves 6, allowing 1 egg per person. Serve with toast or hot buttered muffins.

VEGETABLES AND SALADS

ELI'S SALAD NICOISE

1 can (7 oz) white meat tuna fish
1 jar (7 oz) Italian roasted sweet peppers, cut into strips
1 can (4 oz) eggplant caponata
1 can (1 lb) jumbo pitted black olives
1 can (2 oz) flat anchovy fillets, drained
4 eggs, hard cooked and cut into quarters
2 slices red onion, separated into rings

Empty contents of tuna fish can directly onto the center of a serving platter. Arrange remaining ingredients on the platter. Cover with plastic wrap and refrigerate. A half hour before serving, remove from refrigerator and allow to come to room temperature.

Serves 8 to 10.

CONFETTI COLE SLAW

1 small head cabbage, shredded
1 carrot, pared and grated
1 green pepper, chopped
2 T onion, chopped
1/2 C mayonnaise salad dressing
1/4 C milk
2 T sugar
1/4 tsp salt
1/4 tsp seasoned pepper

Toss vegetables together in a salad bowl. In a small mixing bowl combine mayonnaise, milk, sugar, salt, and seasoned pepper. Pour over vegetables and toss lightly until thoroughly mixed.

Serves 8 to 10.

FRENCH TOSSED SALAD

1 head lettuce
1/2 head chickory
1 bunch watercress
3 tomatoes, cut into wedges
1 red onion, thinly sliced
1 cucumber, thinly sliced
1 can (2 oz) flat anchovy fillets, drained
1 C French dressing
1/4 C mayonnaise
1/4 C Roquefort cheese, crumbled

Wash the salad greens and pat dry. Tear into bite-sized pieces and place in a salad bowl. Add tomatoes, onion, and cucumber. Cut anchovy fillets into small pieces and add to salad bowl. In a separate bowl combine the French dressing and mayonnaise. Fold in the cheese and blend well. Just before serving, pour salad dressing over the salad and toss lightly.

Serves 8.

TOSSED BALKAN SALAD

6 C mixed salad greens, torn into bite-sized pieces
1 C plain yogurt
1/4 C French dressing
1/2 tsp garlic salt
1 T sugar

Place greens in a salad bowl. Mix yogurt, French dressing, garlic salt, and sugar in a mixing bowl. Just before serving, pour mixture over the salad greens and toss well.

Serves 6 to 8.

FOUR-WAY VEGETABLE SALAD

3 packages (3 oz each) lemon-flavored gelatin
2-1/4 C boiling water
1-1/2 T white vinegar
1/2 tsp garlic salt
3 C cold water
1 C carrots, shredded
1 C celery, thinly sliced
1/4 C red pepper, diced
1 C green pepper, diced
1 C canned diced beets, well drained

Dissolve gelatin in boiling water. Add vinegar, garlic salt, and cold water. Put into a 2-1/2 quart mixing bowl. Chill. When thickened but not firm, divide into quarters. Section off one quarter with two small plates and mix in the carrots. Move one plate to section off the next quarter and mix in the celery and red pepper. Move plate to section off the third quarter and mix in the green pepper. Move plate to the last quarter and mix in the beets. Chill until firm. Unmold and garnish with parsley and black olives.

Serves 10.

MARINATED MUSHROOMS

1 lb small fresh mushrooms
1/4 C olive oil
3 T lemon juice
1 garlic clove, halved
1/2 tsp salt
1/8 tsp pepper
1/8 tsp oregano

Remove the stems from the mushrooms. Save stems for soups, stews, or to combine with other vegetables. Wipe caps with a paper towel. Put into a jar. Combine the other ingredients in a saucepan and heat just to the boiling point. Pour over the mushrooms. Cool. Cover and refrigerate for at least 2 days. Shake twice a day. When serving, drain and serve with toothpicks.

Serves 12.

GREEN BEAN AND DILL SALAD

3 pkgs (9 oz each) frozen cut green beans
1/3 C salad oil
3 T wine vinegar
2 tsp dill, minced
1/2 tsp salt
1/4 tsp seasoned pepper

Cook frozen green beans as directed on package. Drain. Add remaining ingredients and mix well. Chill until ready to serve.

Serves 10.

CREAMY CARROT COLE SLAW

2 C carrots, grated
2 C cabbage, finely shredded
1/2 C mayonnaise
3 T milk
1/2 tsp celery seed
1 tsp sugar

Mix carrots and cabbage together. In a small mixing bowl mix the mayonnaise, milk, celery seed, and sugar. Toss with mixed vegetables.

Serves 6 to 8.

PICKLED GREEN BEANS

2 cans (1 lb each) French cut green beans, drained
1/2 C onion, chopped
1/2 C wine vinegar
1/4 C salad oil
1 tsp prepared horseradish
1/2 tsp garlic salt
1 T sugar
1/4 tsp allspice
1/4 tsp dry mustard

In a large saucepan combine the beans with the onion. In a screw-top jar combine the vinegar, horseradish, oil, and seasonings. Shake vigorously. Pour over the beans, bring to a boil, and simmer for 5 minutes, stirring occasionally. Place in a covered container and refrigeratre until serving time.

Serves 8.

HOT GERMAN POTATO SALAD

10 medium potatoes, boiled in their skins
8 slices bacon, diced
2 medium onions, diced
3/4 C sugar
2 tsp dry mustard
2 eggs, beaten
3/4 C vinegar
Salt to taste
Pepper to taste
4 eggs, hard cooked and sliced
2 T parsley, chopped

Peel and cube the potatoes and put in an ovenware bowl or casserole. Fry bacon. Remove bacon from pan and reserve. Fry onions in bacon fat until tender, but not browned. Mix sugar and mustard together. Add to onions in frying pan. Add the beaten eggs and vinegar to onion mixture and cook until thickened, stirring constantly. Pour over the potatoes. Add salt and pepper to taste. Add reserved bacon and egg slices. Mix lightly. Heat in a 250° F. oven for 30 minutes or until ready to serve. Sprinkle parsley on top.

Serves 8 to 10.

MOCHA SPANISH CREAM

1 envelope (1 T) unflavored gelatin
6 T sugar
2 T instant coffee
2 T cocoa
2 eggs, separated
2 C milk
1 tsp vanilla extract
1 T Kahlua or other coffee-flavored liqueur
3 T sliced almonds

Combine gelatin, 2 tablespoons of the sugar, instant coffee and cocoa in saucepan. Beat together egg yolks and milk. Pour into gelatin mixture and stir until blended. Place over low heat and stir constantly until gelatin dissolves and mixture thickens slightly, about 3 to 5 minutes. Remove from heat and stir in vanilla extract and Kahlua. Cool in refrigerator stirring occasionally, until mixture mounds slightly when dropped from the spoon. Beat egg whites until stiff but not dry. Gradually add remaining 4 T sugar, and beat until very stiff. Fold in gelatin mixture. Pour into 4-cup mold. Chill until firm. Unmold and garnish with sliced almonds.

Serves 6 to 8.

ROSE WINE GELATIN

2 envelopes (1 T each) unflavored gelatin
1 C cold water
1 C sugar
2 C Rose wine
3 T lemon juice
1 C heavy cream, whipped

Sprinkle gelatin over water in saucepan. Let stand for 5 minutes until gelatin softens. Place over low heat and stir constantly until gelatin dissolves. Add sugar and continue stirring until sugar dissolves. Remove from heat. Stir in wine and lemon juice. Pour into 4 cup heart-shaped mold. Chill until firm. Unmold and garnish with whipped cream.

Serves 6 to 8.

CANTALOUPE KIRSCH

1 large cantaloupe
1 pint fresh strawberries
1 pint fresh blueberries
1/4 lb seedless green grapes
2 T sugar
1/2 C Kirsch

Seed cantaloupe and cut into balls. Wash and hull strawberries. Wash and remove stems from blueberries. Wash grapes. Combine all fruit with sugar and Kirsch in a bowl and mix thoroughly. Cover and refrigerate at least 2 hours. Stir occasionally.

Serves 8 to 10.

VEGETABLE CASSEROLE AMANDINE

2 pkgs (10 oz each) mixed vegetables frozen in butter sauce, in
  boiling bag
1-1/2 C uncooked egg noodles
1/4 C onion, chopped
1/4 C celery, chopped
1 can (8 oz) tomato sauce
1/2 C sour cream
1/4 C slivered almonds

Cook vegetables in boiling water as directed on package.
Cook noodles in boiling salted water as directed on package to
medium firm. Drain noodles. Partially open boiling bags of
vegetables and drain butter sauce into small frying pan. Sauté
onion and celery in the butter sauce until tender. Combine
cooked noodles and mixed vegetables with onion-celery
mixture. Add tomato sauce and sour cream. Pour into a 1-1/2
quart casserole and top with almonds. Bake in 350°F. oven for
30 minutes.

Serves 10 to 12.

BOHEMIAN SAUERKRAUT

1 can (29 oz) sauerkraut
1 C beer
1/4 tsp caraway seeds

Drain sauerkraut, rince in cold water and drain again. In 1-
1/2 quart casserole combine the sauerkraut, beer and caraway
seeds. Cover and bake in 375°F. oven for 30 minutes.

Serves 8.

FETTUCINI

1 pkg (8 oz) fettucini or egg noodles
1 pkg (8 oz) cream cheese
1/2 lb butter
1/2 C noodle cooking water
1/2 tsp salt
1/4 tsp pepper
1/2 T sugar
1/2 C Parmesan or Romano cheese, grated

Cook fettucini or egg noodles according to directions on package. While noodles are cooking melt the cream cheese and butter over a low flame. Drain noodles and add 1/2 C of the hot water to the cream cheese mixture. Add salt, pepper and sugar to the sauce. Toss the noodles and sauce together in serving dish. Top with grated cheese.

Serves 6.

SWEET POTATO AND APPLE CASSEROLE

3 sweet potatoes, medium sized
4 apples, medium sized, pared and cored
1/2 C brown sugar
1/2 tsp salt
3 T butter
1/4 tsp allspice
1/4 C water

Cook the sweet potatoes in boiling water until tender. Cool and peel. Cut the sweet potatoes and apples into slices, and place in alternate layers in a greased baking dish. Sprinkle each layer with sugar and salt, dot top with butter, dust with allspice, add water and cover. Bake in a 350° F. oven for 30 minutes. Uncover, and bake for an additional 15 minutes.

Serves 6 to 8.

CREAMED SPINACH

2 pkgs frozen spinach, chopped
1/3 C sour cream
1/2 tsp nutmeg

Cook spinach following directions on package. Drain well. Stir in sour cream and transfer to a heated serving dish. Dust with nutmeg.

Serves 8 to 10.

BROILED TOMATOES

4 large, firm tomatoes
4 T butter
1 tsp oregano
Salt to taste
Pepper to taste
1/2 C grated Parmesan cheese

Cut tomatoes in half and place in aluminum foil in broiler pan. Dot with butter, season with oregano, salt and pepper. Sprinkle with Parmesan cheese and broil lightly about 5 minutes or until cheese melts.

Serves 8.

CHILLED VEGETABLES RIVIERA

1 jar (12 oz) white asparagus tips
2 jars (4 oz each) marinated artichoke hearts
2 jars (5-1/2 oz each) marinated mushrooms
5 T Italian salad dressing

Drain all vegetables, reserving 3 T of artichoke marinade. Arrange asparagus tips on serving platter in wheel spoke fashion, tips pointing out. Pile artichokes in the center. Arrange mushrooms between the spokes. Sprinkle lightly with the 3 T artichoke marinade, cover with plastic wrap and refrigerate. Drizzle salad dressing over vegetables just before serving.

Serves 6.

BAKED BARLEY

1/2 C butter
1 medium onion, chopped
2 C barley
4 C chicken bouillon
1/2 tsp salt
1/2 tsp pepper
1 tsp parsley flakes

Melt butter in a skillet. Sauté onion until golden. Add barley and cook, stirring constantly, until barley is golden. Transfer to a casserole and add remaining ingredients. Mix thoroughly and cover tightly. Bake in a 325°F. oven for 30 minutes or until barley is tender.

Serves 8 to 10.

HONEY GLAZED BEETS

1 can (16 oz) sliced beets, drained
3 T lemon juice
1 tsp lemon rind, grated
1/2 tsp salt
1/2 C honey
2 T butter

Arrange beets in heatproof, shallow serving dish. Sprinkle with lemon juice, rind and salt. Pour honey over all and dot with butter. Cover and bake in 350°F. oven for 15 minutes, or until glaze is slightly browned.

Serves 4.

CANDIED CARROTS

1 dozen medium carrots
Boiling salted water
1/2 C butter
1/2 C brown sugar, firmly packed
1/2 tsp allspice

Scrape carrots and cut into julienne strips. Cook in boiling salted water for 10 minutes, or until tender. Drain well. Melt butter, add sugar and allspice. Stir until well blended. Place carrots in ovenproof dish. Pour butter sauce over carrots and bake in 350°F. oven for 15 minutes.

Serves 8.

BROCCOLI ITALIAN

3 pkgs frozen broccoli spears
2 T olive oil
4 T butter
1 clove garlic
3/4 grated Parmesan cheese

Partly defrost broccoli. In a large skillet heat the olive oil and butter. Cut garlic in half and sauté until golden. Remove the garlic and spread the broccoli in a single layer in the pan. Sauté, turning gently, for 10 minutes, or until tender. Arrange in a flameproof serving dish. Sprinkle with cheese and place under broiler for about 1 minute.

Serves 6 to 8.

BREADS

BUFFET BREAD

1 long loaf French or Italian bread
1/2 C butter
1/4 C parsley, finely chopped
1/4 C green onion, finely chopped

Cut bread lengthwise, but not all the way through. Soften butter and mix in parsley and green onion. Spread mixture in center of bread. Close bread and wrap in aluminum foil. Bake in a 400°F. oven for 10 minutes or until butter melts. Slice and serve warm.

Serves 6.

THREE GRAIN BREAD

1 C corn meal
1 C rye flour
1 C graham flour
2 tsp baking soda
1 tsp salt
1/8 tsp allspice
3/4 C molasses
1-3/4 C sour milk
1/4 C cream

Put dry ingredients in a large mixing bowl and mix well. In a separate bowl place the molasses, sour milk and cream. Stir until well blended. Pour liquid slowly into dry mixture. Stir only until well moistened. Pour batter into well-greased 9-inch loaf pan and bake in 350°F. oven for 1 hour and 15 minutes, or until done. Cool thoroughly before slicing.

Serves 12.

ITALIAN GARLIC BREAD

1/2 C butter, softened
2 garlic cloves, halved
1/2 C Italian cheese, grated
1 loaf French or Italian bread

Cream butter. Pierce garlic halves with toothpick. Submerge garlic in butter. Let stand for one half hour, stirring occasionally. Remove garlic and add the grated cheese to garlic butter. Slice bread not quite through in 1-inch slices. Spread the slices with the garlic butter. Wrap aluminum foil around bread and bake in hot oven, 400°F., until butter and cheese mixture melts, about 10 minutes. Serve hot.

Serves 6.

HIGHLAND SCONES

2 C flour
4 tsp baking powder
1/2 tsp salt
1/4 C butter, softened
2 eggs, beaten
6 T milk

Sift flour, baking powder and salt twice. Add the butter, eggs and milk. Mix just until thoroughly moistened. Turn onto well floured board and knead 10 times. Roll out 1/2 inch thick. Cut into small rounds, about 2 to 2-1/2 inches. Place on greased cookie sheet and bake in preheated oven at 400°F. for 12 to 15 minutes. Serve with butter and marmalade.

Makes about 36 scones.

GINA'S CRANBERRY NUT LOAF

2 C flour
1 tsp baking soda
1 tsp salt
3 T vinegar, plus water to make a total of 2/3 C
1 egg
3/4 C sugar
1/4 C salad oil
1/3 C orange juice, fresh or frozen
1 tsp grated orange rind
1 C chopped cranberries
1 C nuts, chopped (any kind you choose to use)

Sift together the flour, baking soda and salt. Pour the 3 tablespoons of vinegar into a measuring cup. Add water to make a measure of 2/3 cup. Beat egg in a large mixing bowl. Add the sugar, oil, vinegar and water mixture, orange juice, and the orange rind. Mix well. Add the dry ingredients and blend thoroughly. Stir in cranberries and nuts. Grease and line a 5 x 9-inch loaf pan with wax paper. Pour the batter into the pan and bake in a 350° F. oven for 50 minutes or until the loaf tests done.

Serves 12.

PLYMOUTH PUMPKIN BREAD

1-1/2 C sugar
1/2 C vegetable oil
2 eggs
1-2/3 C flour
1/2 tsp cinnamon
3/4 tsp salt
1/2 tsp nutmeg
1 tsp baking soda
1/3 C water
1 C cooked pumpkin, mashed
1/2 C walnuts, chopped

Combine sugar and oil in a large mixing bowl. Add eggs, beating well after each addition. Sift dry ingredients together. Add dry ingredients alternately with water to mixture in the mixing bowl. Add pumpkin and fold in the nuts. Pour batter into a well greased 5 x 9-inch loaf pan. Bake in a 350° F. oven for 50 to 60 minutes, or until loaf tests done. Cool thoroughly before slicing.

Serves 12.

CAPE COD BISCUITS

4 C biscuit mix
1-1/2 C milk
16 tsp whole cranberry sauce

Blend biscuit mix and milk with fork just until thoroughly moistened. Drop from spoon onto lightly greased cookie sheet, making 16 biscuits. With the back of a teaspoon make a small depression in the center of each biscuit. Bake in a 450°F. oven for 10 to 15 minutes, or until biscuits are a golden brown. Just before serving fill depressions in top of biscuits with the cranberry sauce.

Makes 16.

LIMPA MUFFINS

1 egg
1 C rye flour
3/4 C flour
1/4 C brown sugar, firmly packed
4 tsp baking powder
1/2 tsp salt
1-1/2 tsp grated orange peel
3/4 C milk
1/4 C cooking oil
1/4 C molasses

Beat the egg slightly in a large mixing bowl. Add all other ingredients. Mix until just thoroughly moistened. Fill well greased muffin cups about one half full. Bake in 400°F. oven for 15 to 20 minutes or until golden brown.

Makes 12 muffins.

ITALIAN BISCUITS

2 C flour
3 tsp baking powder
1 tsp salt
1/3 C shortening
2/3 C American or Cheddar cheese, shredded
2 T green pepper, finely chopped
1 T pimiento, chopped
3/4 C milk

In a large mixing bowl combine the flour, baking powder and salt. Cut in the shortening until particles are fine. Blend in the cheese, pepper, and the pimiento. Mix well. Add milk; mix only until moistened thoroughly. Knead on floured surface 10 times. Roll out to 1/2-inch thickness and cut into rounds with floured 2-1/4-inch cutter. Place on ungreased cookie sheet. Bake at 450°F. for 15 minutes.

Makes 18 biscuits.

APRICOT CRESCENTS

2 pkgs (8 oz) refrigerated crescent rolls
16 tsp apricot jam
2 T butter, melted
2 T sugar
2 T nuts, chopped fine

Take refrigerated crescent rolls from package. Lay flat. Place 1 tsp apricot jam on wide end. Roll up and bake according to directions on package. Brush with melted butter and sprinkle with sugar and chopped nuts. Serve warm.

Makes 16 rolls.

ORANGE NUT MUFFINS

2 C flour
1/3 C sugar
3 tsp baking powder
1 tsp salt
1/2 C hazelnuts, chopped
1 egg
1/2 C orange juice (fresh or frozen)
1 T grated orange peel
1/2 C orange marmalade
1/4 C milk
1/4 C cooking oil

In a large mixing bowl combine flour, sugar, baking powder, salt, and chopped hazelnuts. Combine egg, orange juice, orange peel, orange marmalade, milk and oil. Add to dry ingredients. Mix only until evenly moistened. Do not overmix. Fill paper lined muffin cups 2/3 full and set aside.

TOPPING:

1/4 C sugar
1 T flour
1 T butter, softened
1/2 tsp cinnamon

In a small mixing bowl combine all the topping ingredients. Sprinkle topping over muffin batter. Bake at 400° F. for 20 to 25 minutes, or until muffins are golden brown and test done.

Makes 12 muffins.

CRUNCHY TOAST STICKS

4 slices white bread, toasted
1/3 C corn flake crumbs
1/4 C grated Romano cheese
1/2 tsp onion salt
1/3 C butter, softened

Remove crust from toast slices. Cut each slice into 4 long sticks. Combine corn flake crumbs with cheese. Mix onion salt with butter. Roll each toast stick first in the butter and then in the corn flake-cheese mixture. Just before serving, place on an ungreased cookie sheet and bake in 400° F. oven for 5 minutes, or until crisp.

Makes 16 sticks.

CRUNCHY CARAWAY STICKS

2 C flour
3 tsp baking powder
1 tsp salt
4 T sugar
1/2 C shortening
1 T caraway seeds
3/4 C milk

Sift together the flour, baking powder, salt, and sugar. Cut in the shortening until the mixture is the consistency of cornmeal. Add the caraway seeds and enough milk to give the dough the consistency of a biscuit dough. Knead on a lightly floured board 6 times. Roll out 1/4 inch thick. Cut into strips 4 inches long and 1/4 inch wide. Place on a lightly greased cookie sheet and bake at 375° F. for 10 minutes or until a light brown.

Makes about 20 sticks.

DESSERTS

DONNA'S HOT FUDGE DELIGHT

2 (3 oz) chocolate bars with almonds
2 T cream
1 T orange-flavored liqueur (or rum)
6 slices plain pound cake
6 large scoops ice cream
3 T slivered almonds

Melt chocolate bars in top of double boiler. When melted blend in cream and the liqueur. Keep warm over hot water. Toast cake. Put cake on individual serving plates. Put ice cream on top of cake slices. Pour hot fudge sauce over all and top with slivered almonds.

Serves 6.

PINEAPPLE ISLAND DELIGHT

1 can (1 lb 14 oz) pineapple slices
1/4 C butter
1 C apricot-pineapple preserves
1/2 C rum
8 scoops vanilla or pineapple ice cream (about 1 qt)
2 T crystalized ginger, minced

Drain pineapple and reserve 6 tablespoons of the syrup. Melt butter in large frying pan, add pineapple slices and sauté until lightly browned. Stir in reserved pineapple syrup and apricot-pineapple preserves. Heat and stir gently until pineapple looks glazed. Warm rum im small pan over low heat. Pour rum over pineapple slices in pan and ignite. Put ice cream scoops in individual serving dishes. When flames die down stir sauce gently. Arrange pineapple slices around ice cream. Pour hot sauce over all, and garnish with ginger.

Serves 8.

CHERRIES JUBILEE

1 can (1 lb, 4 oz) pitted Bing cherries
1 T cornstarch
1 T cold water
1 qt vanilla ice cream
1/2 C cherry-flavored brandy

Drain juice from cherries and reserve 1/2 cup. In a saucepan stir cornstarch and water until cornstarch is dissolved. Add cherry juice and cook over low heat, stirring constantly, until sauce thickens slightly. Add cherries and warm through. Transfer cherry sauce to serving dish or a chafing dish. Spoon ice cream into individual dessert dishes. Warm brandy slightly and pour over the cherry sauce. Ignite and ladle over ice cream while still flaming.

Serves 6 to 8.

FESTIVE FRUIT DESSERT

1 pkg (8 oz) cream cheese
1/4 C Marsala wine
1/2 C heavy cream, whipped
1 pkg (4 oz) candied mixed fruit
Assorted fresh fruit (apple slices, pineapple slices, pear wedges, melon wedges or balls, orange segments)

Soften cream cheese and beat in Marsala wine. Fold in whipped cream and candied fruit. Arrange fresh fruit attractively on large platter and serve with fruit dip. May be eaten with the fingers.

Serves 8 to 10.

CHAMPAGNE FRUIT PUNCH

1 bottle champagne
1/2 C apricot brandy
1 orange, peeled and sliced thin
1/2 C crushed pineapple
1/2 C sliced strawberries
2 T powdered sugar

Combine all ingredients in punch bowl with a block of ice, or a block of frozen orange juice.

Makes about 20 servings.

PARTY PUNCH

1 qt strong tea
1 qt rye whiskey
1 pt dark rum
1 pt orange juice
1 C lemon juice
1 qt apple juice

Combine all ingredients in a punch bowl with a block of ice. Freeze fresh fruit such as pineapple slices, orange slices, and cherries in the freezing tray for an attractive ice block.

Makes about 25 punch cups.

KENTUCKY EGGNOG

2 dozen eggs, separated
2-1/2 C bourbon
1 qt heavy cream
6 T sugar
1 C (additional) sugar
Nutmeg to taste

In a large mixing bowl of electric mixer beat egg yolks for 20 minutes, until they are light and very fluffy. Continue beating and add bourbon *very* slowly. This may be done the night before and kept in the refrigerator in a covered container. Just before serving whip the cream until it stands in peaks, then add the 6 tablespoons sugar. Lightly fold in egg yolk mixture. Whip egg whites until they are dry and stand in peaks. Add the 1 cup sugar, one tablespoon at a time, and continue beating for 10 minutes after last spoonful of sugar has been added. Fold egg whites into the egg yolk mixture and blend until well mixed and smooth. Top each cup with a dash of nutmeg.

Makes 30 servings.

COCONUT CREAM PIE

1 9-inch baked pie shell
5 eggs, separated
1-1/4 cups granulated sugar
1/4 teaspoon salt
1/4 cup cornstarch
2-3/4 cups milk
2 teaspoons vanilla
1/4 cup butter
1 10-ounce can grated moist coconut
1/4 cup (additional) granulated sugar

Beat the yolks until light and lemon colored. Set aside. Mix the sugar, salt and cornstarch together thoroughly. Scald the milk in the top of a double boiler. Add the sugar mixture to the milk and beat until free of lumps. Add three tablespoons of the hot milk mixture to the egg yolks, mix and then add the yolks to the hot milk. Beat again until thoroughly mixed. Cook over boiling water, stirring constantly, until the mixture has thickened and coats the spoon. Remove from the heat and allow to cool slightly.

Mix the vanilla and the butter together. Add 3/4 of the can of coconut and mix very well. (Reserve the remaining coconut for the meringue topping.) Stir the coconut mixture into the milk mixture. When blended, pour into the baked pie shell.

Beat the egg whites until they begin to stand in peaks. Gradually add the additional 1/4 cup sugar and continue beating until the mixture stands in firm peaks. Cover the pie with the meringue, making sure you bring it out to the edges, completely sealing and covering the custard. Sprinkle the remaining 1/4 can of coconut over the top of the meringue. Bake in a 325°F. oven for 20 minutes or until the top has turned a golden brown. Cool before cutting. Serves 6.

LEMON PIE

1 9-inch baked pie shell
2 cups milk
1 cup granulated sugar
1/4 teaspoon salt
1/4 cup cornstarch
3 eggs, separated
1 tablespoon grated lemon rind
1/4 cup lemon juice
1/4 cup (additional) granulated sugar

Scald the milk in the top of a double boiler; allow to cool slightly. Mix the sugar, salt and cornstarch together thoroughly. Add to the scalded milk; beat with a whisk or rotary beater until free of lumps. Cook over rapidly boiling water, stirring constantly, for 10 minutes or until the mixture has thickened and begins to coat a spoon.

Beat the egg yolks until they are light and lemon colored. Take several spoonfuls of the milk mixture and add it to the egg yolks; then mix the yolks into the thickened mixture. Beat for a second or so to mix well. Cook, stirring constantly, for 5 additional minutes. Remove from the heat and add the lemon rind and lemon juice, mix well. Allow to cool for 5 minutes and then pour into the baked pie shell.

Beat the egg whites until they stand in peaks. Gradually add the additional 1/4 cup sugar and beat again. Using a rubber spoon, spread the meringue over the lemon pie filling. Bring to the edges of the crust, sealing the filling all the way around.

Place in a 325°F. oven for 15 to 20 minutes or until the peaks of the meringue begin to turn a golden brown. Cool to room temperature before cutting. Serves 6.

2-EGG THIN COOKIES

1 cup margarine, at room temperature, or half margarine and
  half butter
1 cup granulated sugar
2 eggs
1 cup plus 2 tablespoons all-purpose flour
1/2 teaspoon vanilla
1/2 teaspoon lemon extract

Cream the margarine and the sugar together until light and
fluffy. Beat the eggs until they are light and lemon colored and
then mix with the margarine and the sugar.

Add the flour, vanilla and lemon extract and mix thoroughly.

Using a teaspoon, drop on a well greased cookie sheet. Bake
at 375°F. for 8 minutes or until the edges are just beginning to
turn brown. Makes 8 dozen thin cookies.

EGG AND HONEY SQUARES

4 eggs
1 cup honey
1-1/3 cups all-purpose flour
1 teaspoon baking powder
1/4 teaspoon salt
1 cup English walnuts, coarsely chopped
1 cup pitted dates, coarsely chopped
2 teaspoons vanilla
1 cup powdered sugar

Beat the eggs until they are light and bubbly. While still
beating, add the honey and continue to beat for a few seconds
longer.

Mix the flour, baking powder and salt together thoroughly
and gradually add to the egg and honey mixture, beating after
each addition. Add the walnuts and the dates and mix all well.
Stir in the vanilla.

Place in a well buttered baking tin. The depth of the mixture
should be about 1/4 inch; use two tins if necessary. Bake in a
350°F. oven for 12 to 15 minutes or until the center is firm to the
touch. Remove from the oven and allow to cool slightly. Cut
into 2-inch squares. Roll the squares in the powdered sugar
while still slightly warm. Yield: 36 squares.

Note: These squares will keep for weeks if wrapped tightly in
aluminum foil and stored in an air-tight container.